More Than a Methodist

The Life and Ministry of Donald English
The Authorised Biography

More Than a Methodist

The Life and Ministry of Donald English
The Authorised Biography

Brian Hoare and Ian Randall

PATERNOSTER PRESS

Paternoster Press is an imprint of Authentic Media,
P.O. Box 300, Carlisle, Cumbria, CA3 0QS, UK
and
P.O. Box 1047, Waynesboro, GA 30830-2047, USA

Website: www.paternoster-publishing.com

British Library Cataloguing in Publication Data
A catalogue record for this book is available from the British Library

ISBN 1-84227-203-9

Cover Design by FourNineZero
Typeset by WestKey Ltd, Falmouth, Cornwall
Printed in Great Britain by Cox & Wyman, Reading, Berkshire

' "More Than a Methodist" sums up the life and work of Donald English perfectly – a fitting tribute to a great Christian man and leader. Donald defied pigeonholing. He was his own man, because he was first Christ's. It is my hope that this biography will enable Donald's sparkling, human and Christ-centred life to challenge us all to be faithful servants of the Lord he followed.'

Lord Carey of Clifton
Former Archbishop of Canterbury

'This admirable biography covers every aspect of a remarkable and many-faceted life. Donald English's ministry was owned and valued by people of many denominations. He was, to use a title usually applied to the Bishop of Rome, a pontiff, a bridge – a builder of bridges of understanding between Christians with different theological perspectives. This dimension of his ministry is fully explored and it has lessons for all who are committed to the cause of Christian unity.'

The Revd Dr Kenneth Greet
Former President and Secretary of the Methodist Conference and a past Chairperson of the World Methodist Council

'Donald English's contribution to the national life of the British Church in the late twentieth century was incalculable. I am so glad that at last we have a scholarly yet personal appraisal of his life. It not only makes fascinating reading for those of us who knew Don and worked with him, but it provides the kind of inspiration and encouragement which the emerging generation of church leaders so desperately needs. I warmly commend it.'

The Revd Dr Rob Frost
Director, Share Jesus International

'Donald English was one of the greatest men of God I have ever known. His arms were wide open to the fellowship of all believers, whatever their denominational background. There are very few men in the ministry of any denomination that I looked up to and wanted to emulate like Don English. He was an evangelist at heart, as well as a great teacher and pastor.'

Dr Billy Graham

Contents

Foreword

*The Rt. Revd and Rt. Hon. The Lord Carey of Clifton
(former Archbishop of Canterbury)*

'More Than a Methodist' sums up the life and work of Donald English perfectly. And yet he was a clear Methodist – shaped by that great tradition and proud of it. From its rich reservoirs of Christian orthodoxy, biblical preaching and holiness of life, Donald grew to an impressive stature and became a gifted evangelist and Christian leader.

But Donald was not the kind of man one could easily categorise. Yes, he was an evangelical who was at home with all evangelicals, yet there was a generosity of spirit that transcended a party spirit. He was able to see Jesus Christ in Catholic and Orthodox traditions and feel at home with Christians of different persuasions. Yes, he was a Bible man, but no one could ever hurl the epithet 'fundamentalist' at him; he was only too well aware of the importance of depth and analysis when it came to interpreting Scripture. Yes, he was keen to reform human structures, but he was only too well aware of the hardness of the human heart which made the task of the gospel penetrating politics and society a far from easy one. In short, Donald defied pigeon-holing. He was his own man – because he was first Christ's.

I recall attending the remarkable United Methodist Conference in Cleveland, Ohio, shortly after Donald's death. It was a huge gathering of Methodists from around the world. In my address I spoke of the friendship Donald and I shared, and I paid a tribute to his remarkable gifts. I then went on to reflect on the experience of meeting such a leader in the context of the difficulties of reconciling Anglican and Methodist theologies of ministry. I remarked: 'It is impossible for me to consider a fellow minister such as Donald as somehow lacking in grace because he was ordained a Methodist and I was ordained an Anglican!' The vast audience rose as one and cheered as I affirmed Donald as a humble man of God, chosen just as I had been to serve the same Lord. To be sure, the issue of the historic episcopate has to be addressed by both churches, but no progress can be made if either church regards the other as somehow less apostolic, orthodox or lacking in grace.

I congratulate Brian Hoare and Ian Randall on presenting us with a fitting tribute to a great Christian man and leader. Donald was certainly 'more than a Methodist' because he belonged to us all. It is my hope that this biography will enable Donald's sparkling, human and Christ-centred life to challenge us all to be faithful servants of the Lord he followed.

George Carey

Authors' Preface and Acknowledgements

The death of Donald English on 28 August 1998 inflicted a heavy loss on the Christian world. He had retired only three years previously and could have been expected to have continued his effective ministry as a Methodist and ecumenical statesman for many years. Donald English's life and work were many faceted. He was an outstanding Methodist preacher whose gifts were used in local church ministry, in overseas mission and at many significant large-scale events. He was also a superb chairperson and organiser who brought wisdom and guidance to many challenging situations within Methodist life. But Donald English was more than a Methodist. From his early period as a Christian leader he identified with the wider Christian world. His contribution to evangelicalism and wider Christian life and thought was considerable. Increasingly during his ministry he was recognised as an evangelist who was able to serve within ecumenical contexts. This book attempts to pay tribute to the varied aspects of Donald's career. He will be referred to in the book as Donald or Donald English, rather than English, since this usage seems to be best fitted both to the style of the writing and to his own personality.

This biography traces, firstly, Donald English's early life in the north-east of England, where he was born in 1930, and especially the way in which Methodism shaped his future. His time as a university student and then as someone involved in ministry to students is examined in the second chapter. In 1960 Donald embarked on theological teaching, but two years later he and his wife, Bertha, went overseas, to work for four years in Nigeria. This period of missionary service is dealt with in some detail. A chapter is devoted to the period 1966 to 1972, when Donald was a Methodist circuit minister in Cullercoats. The next chapter outlines Donald's work as a Methodist theological teacher from 1960 to 1962 and again from 1972 to 1982. Under the chapter heading 'Methodist Leader', Donald's work as General Secretary of the Methodist Home Mission Division from 1982 to 1995 and his two periods as President of the Methodist Conference are outlined, together with his leadership of evangelicals in Methodism. Donald's preaching, for which he was renowned, is the subject of a further chapter. This is followed by a chapter containing an analysis of his ecumenical contribution. Two chapters cover Donald's substantial international role. The final chapter is an evaluation of Donald English as a person. Since this is a Christian biography, rather than a scholarly study, footnotes have been included only where it was judged they would be of interest to the general reader.

This book is a fully co-operative effort. One of the authors is a Methodist minister who was a friend and colleague of Donald's and the other is a Baptist tutor who is a church historian with a particular interest in evangelicalism. Our hope is that between us we are able to offer perspectives that will be of interest within World Methodism and also within the wider Christian community. In a number of significant ways the life of Donald English illuminates developments in the Christian church, especially in the West, in the second half of the twentieth century.

Writing the biography of someone whose life touched so many thousands of people, embraced so many different denominations and reached so many different countries would not have been possible without the help of a very large number of people. First and foremost, we are grateful to Richard and Paul English, Donald's two sons, who have given the project their enthusiastic backing from its inception and have provided much valuable background information. Secondly, two personal friends of Donald English from his early days, Graham Turner and Ronald Abbott, have devoted considerable time and energy to this book, forming a small working group together with the authors to plan its contents and monitor its progress, reading each chapter as it was written and suggesting improvements and additions. Thirdly, the work would have been so much more difficult to accomplish without the financial support of Charles and Mary K. Turkington, two of Donald's American friends at Lake Junaluska, and generous gifts from anonymous donors. These enabled us to undertake the travel and correspondence necessary at the research stage.

Donald English was a very organised person and filed away a great deal of what crossed his desk, so a huge amount of material had accumulated by the time of his death. We are indebted to Robert Bates, Chaplain at the Westminster Institute of Education, Oxford, for storing the many boxes of papers containing that material and allowing us to use his home to sort through them, and to Peter Greetham, who gave valuable assistance in that process. We are gratified that the papers worthy of being retained (still a significant number) have, through the good offices of Peter Forsaith, become a permanent part of the archives at the Wesley Centre, Oxford.

Much of what is in this book has come from personal memories rather than filed papers, however, and we acknowledge the help of the many people who have contributed in that way. Nigel Waterfield helpfully arranged a meeting of some of Donald's relatives and boyhood friends in Consett, where valuable memories were shared, and memories were contributed in a similar way at a meeting in Cullercoats of those who remembered Donald's ministry there, arranged by Bert and Win Lever. In response to a request in the Christian press for memories and stories of Donald English, a large number of people wrote, e-mailed or telephoned, and we gladly acknowledge the invaluable contribution they have made to the contents of this book. Many of them are named in the text and their comments directly quoted, but those whose names do not appear in print also helped greatly to build up the total picture of the life described in these pages. Others were kind enough to respond readily to our specific requests for information, and among them we are especially grateful to Brian Beck, John A. Newton, Peter Stephens, John Barratt, Sunday Mbang, David Bridge, Irene Bower, Peter Sutcliffe, David Mullins, David King, John B. Taylor, Geoff Johnston, Betty Ross, Kenneth Cracknell, Jill Edmonds and Esmond ('Jeff') Jefferies. George Morris and Eddie Fox contributed valuable material on the international front, and we are particularly indebted to Joe Hale for all his assistance over researching the two chapters on World Methodism.

The editor of the *Methodist Recorder* was most helpful in allowing access to archive material from that paper. We are grateful to Churches' Television Centre and Cliff College Recordings for the use of transcribed extracts from their productions. We acknowledge also our indebtedness to the editor, authors and publisher (Moorleys) of the only other publication so far to have been written about our subject:

Donald English: An Evangelical Celebration. Our work is indebted to that series of essays.

Invaluable assistance both with transcribing recorded contributions and typing up written material has been provided by Valerie Castle (who served for a time as Donald English's Correspondence Secretary) and Christine Donald, and we are grateful also to Joyce Hoare for her work on the index. Lucy Atherton and Jill Morris of Paternoster Press have offered much help as the book has progressed towards publication.

It is our hope that this book will not only do justice to the memory of Donald English but will also be of help to those looking for renewed spiritual vision in the twenty-first century. There is evidence of the continuing impact of Donald English's life and ministry in this respect. David Coffey, the General Secretary of the Baptist Union, during his induction address as Moderator of the Free Churches on 12 March 2003, spoke of 'what my late friend Donald English used to term "God's free samples" '. David Coffey based part of his address on Donald's words, arguing for a ministry that offered the world some 'free samples' of faith, of hope, of gospel love, of radical discipleship and of peace making. Donald's own vision of ministry was that it was 'uncertain, patchy, sometimes tempestuous, but certainly exciting and demanding'. He embodied this in his own story, and it is that story which we have sought to convey.

Brian Hoare, Knaresborough, North Yorkshire
Ian Randall, Spurgeon's College, London

Easter 2003

Introduction

Joe Hale

I first met Donald English at the 1976 World Methodist Conference in Dublin, and he became a trusted friend and constant example I learned from and sought to emulate for the next twenty-two years until his untimely death in 1998. I am glad to have the opportunity of commending this account of his life and work to what I hope will be a wide readership. The qualities of character, commitment and compassion I came to admire so much myself extended to everyone he met, and I hope that this book will not only bring the challenge of Donald's life in fresh ways to those who knew him, but also introduce him to a new generation who did not.

Donald English literally catapulted into the world arena through four Bible studies he presented to the Thirteenth World Methodist Conference in 1976 when he was forty-six years old. Early-morning studies at world conferences were often attended only by the most zealous, but after the first morning in Dublin the arena was packed! That conference in Ireland introduced Donald to World Methodism. It was more than his ability as a speaker that attracted people, however. He possessed keen insight into the Scriptures and the unusual ability to communicate what he had discovered in ways that gripped people's attention. His comprehensive grasp of the Christian faith was matched by his skill in presenting its claims in an interesting and forceful way, bringing fresh insights and an attractive contemporary application. Besides all this, he was a caring person, and always a gentleman!

Donald English also lived what he taught and was able, first in Britain and then across the world, to convince Christians that they must do more to make the faith understandable and inviting. He cared deeply for people – all people! He believed that the church, and individual Christians, could do better in presenting Jesus Christ to sceptical and unbelieving people, and often spoke of our being 'alongside' those we wished to come to know Christ. The discipline of 'Christian apologetics', making the case for the faith to such persons, was something he did very well, and he profoundly challenged the rest of us in this area. Indeed, it was from Donald English that I first heard the words 'Christian apologetics'.

At the time of his death Donald was a formidable world figure, known and respected by millions of persons over the world. He had met many heads of state, including P.W. Botha and F.W. de Klerk in South Africa; he had lunched with Her Majesty Queen Elizabeth at Buckingham Palace; he was invited to a private audience with His Holiness Pope John Paul II at the Vatican. Leaders of other Christian world communions knew and respected him, as did thousands of Methodist Christians in such far-flung places as Seoul, Rio de Janeiro, Lagos, Mexico City, Nairobi, Hong Kong, Estonia and Bulgaria, Kuala Lumpur, Jakarta, Sydney, Jerusalem – not to mention many cities in the United States and across Europe.

This biography, *More than a Methodist*, tells the story of the 'more'! It is a present invitation and challenge to all of us to look closely at what one person did when he walked into our lives and, by his own life, challenged us to be 'more than

xviii   *Introduction*

we are'. I am especially pleased that Brian Hoare, Donald's close friend and colleague and one of those who knew him best, has collaborated with a Baptist writer, Ian Randall (for Donald was more than a Methodist), in opening up his remarkable and insightful life and work to us all.

Joe Hale
General Secretary 1976–2001
World Methodist Council

1

North-East Roots

What turned out to be a remarkable life began in very unremarkable surroundings. Donald English was born on 20 July 1930 at High Westwood, a close-knit mining community in Consett, County Durham, his parents, Robert and Ena English, both coming from mining stock. Donald's mother had lived with her grandparents, Sarah and John Turnbull, and her uncle, John Thompson, at Victoria Terrace, Hamsterley Colliery, until her marriage to Bob, who was a colliery electrician. This north-eastern mining community was thus an important part of Donald's background. So too was Methodism. John Turnbull, Donald's step-great-grandfather, had been a Methodist local preacher. Donald's parents regularly took Donald with them to worship at High Westwood Methodist Church (closed in September 1963), the church almost opposite their home, and the one to which they had taken him to be baptised as an infant.

It was here that, at the surprisingly early age of three, Donald was allowed to pump the church organ, played by his uncle, George Weston – an experience he loved to recall with a typical touch of humour in his later years. As he described it to a local newspaper in 1979: 'My onerous task was to pump the organ. The effectiveness of this ministry was measured by the descent of a lead weight, what I called my 'mouse'. As it came down I was winning; if it went up, the organist was winning. The competition gave to the services an excitement of a kind rarely matched since!' From the vantage point of the organ pumper's stool, young Donald could view the whole congregation, and he later commented that what impressed him so much in those early years was the fact that the folk he saw in church were the same folk he saw going off to work the next day, or out and about in the shops. Yet here they were each Sunday, offering their worship, saying their prayers and listening to the Word of God.

Donald was an only child, but he had ten cousins living locally, most of whom also came from mining families, and he loved spending time with them. Christmas was a particularly important family time when Donald, his parents, aunts, uncles and cousins would gather on Christmas Eve at Evenwood House, the home of his great-uncle John Thompson and aunt Eleanor, for party games and food. Blind man's buff, musical chairs and pinning the tail on the donkey were particularly popular. On one such occasion Donald, always ready to see the funny side of things, was reduced to fits of laughter by the fact that some indoor fireworks almost wrecked the paper chains.

The 1930s were, however, difficult years in the north-east. These were the days of miners' strikes and the Great Depression, and life was hard for the English family, as for others. Bob English had no less than three serious mining accidents, in one of which an electric current passed through his body, and yet he survived. His skills as an electrician were, fortunately, in demand beyond the pit itself, and electrical odd jobs done for friends and neighbours earned him a few welcome extra shillings. Nevertheless, Donald later recalled the time when his mother had to go to a butcher, who was a cousin of his father, to borrow £5 in order to feed the family.

After some years in High Westwood the family moved to another area of Consett, Leadgate, and later to a small

two-bedroomed terraced bungalow in Leaside, Delves Lane
– two comparatively quick moves, necessitated by Bob
English's work. The Leaside bungalow, which was owned
by Consett Iron Company and transferred to the Coal
Board in 1947, was considered quite well appointed for its
time, since the outside toilet in the back yard had a proper
chain-pull flush. In the 1960s, when the pit closed, Bob and
Ena English took the chance offered by the Coal Board of
buying their home – for the not insignificant sum of £600.
It was around the time of their move to Delves Lane that
Donald's parents fell away from church attendance for a
time, though Donald was still sent to Sunday school. He
recalled how, when he was six years old and his mother was
ill with pleurisy, he was reading a Sunday school prize
about the story of Moses and was moved to tears by the
story. 'I read and re-read the account of his death on
the mountain looking into the Promised Land,' he wrote.
'How much I was crying for Moses and how much for fear
about my mother's illness I can't judge, but that deeply
religious story provided a proper outlet for my emotions
at that time.'

Donald's schooling had begun at what was known
locally as the 'top' junior school, the Delves Lane School,
where he was to be much influenced by the only male
teacher there, Jack Gair, who came from a neighbouring
village. Gair was a strong man, a keen sportsman and a Cub
Scout leader, and Donald and his fellow pupils greatly
admired him. He somehow managed to motivate them to
work hard, and Donald later acknowledged that it was
largely due to Gair that he got into Consett Grammar
School (in those days called 'The Tech'). As he put it: 'When
I passed the 11+ examination it was like the door into
heaven. The first day I wore my little cap and carried my
brand new bag I really felt I had arrived.' It was not long
before Donald began to develop a real interest in history,

and in an address at Cliff College, Derbyshire, many years later, he described how he eventually decided that this was the subject he would pursue:

> If I took you back to Consett where I come from I could take you to Room 5 and to the radiator where I stood and talked to our History Mistress, Miss Wright – whom we very naughtily called Bessie. Bessie Wright talked to me by the radiator about how they taught history at university, and in that moment I knew that I would read history at university. Everything else about my life follows from that particular decision.

Although by now he had moved his church allegiance to the Delves Lane Methodist Sunday school near his home, Donald and a couple of friends also gave the local Anglican church a try for a time, largely because they wanted to sample what went on at their Scout troop. They even went to the lengths of getting confirmed at about the age of thirteen, but soon reverted to their Methodist roots. It was Donald's growing interest in sport, particularly football, which was the motivating factor here.

The 10th North West Durham (Consett) Boys' Brigade Company, based at Middle Street Methodist Church, was looking for someone to play outside right at the time, and one of Donald's friends, Bill Hodgson, who played inside right, encouraged him to join the Boys' Brigade (BB) in order to qualify for the team. He did so, and in both sporting and spiritual terms he never looked back. He played football not only for the BB, but for his class, and eventually for the grammar school team. By the age of sixteen he was playing centre half for Eden Juniors, a local team for lads up to the age of eighteen. Indeed, if he had wished to do so, he had skills that meant he could have played football professionally – but that is a later part of the story. Donald was not always a paragon of virtue on the football field in those days. One person who remembers him at the time commented:

> On the football field he was a completely different person. You would have thought he was a savage. Nobody got past him. He was very competitive. I was a referee in the Boys' Brigade, and if you blew him up for something wrong he wasn't very kind. He could use the lingo like everybody else, and he'd soon tell me where to get off!

As well as being a keen footballer, Donald showed unusual skills as a cricketer: in fact he was a good all-round sportsman. Recalling how he played cricket for the Shotley Bridge eleven, he loved to tell the tale of how he scored his first fifty for that team. The batsman at the other end had been a professional cricketer, and Donald described how when he had played the stroke that brought up his fifty he simply stood at his own end and waited. 'I stood there and made him walk all the way to my end, expecting him to say "Congratulations!" but all he said was "Now take a fresh guard and make another fifty." '

The BB began to exert a strong influence not only on Donald's sporting process, but also on his spiritual development, and he recounted something of that influence in the chapter he contributed to the book *My Call to Preach*:

> Once I had joined [the BB] I discovered much more than football: drill, first-aid and the Bible Class. We were required to attend Bible Class every Sunday before morning service. On the strength of that attendance we were allowed to leave morning worship before the sermon. That seemed to be a fair deal![1]

---

[1] Quotations from *My Call to Preach* are from E. England (ed.), *My Call to Preach* (Crowborough: Highland, 1986), pp. 40–52.

One of Donald's first stirrings towards Christian commitment came as he listened to a man named George Little speak in the Bible class, and George was someone for whom he retained a high regard over many subsequent years. Donald's testimony continues:

> How was I to find a similar faith? There were occasions when I set off to read the Bible right through over a period of months, but I rarely got beyond Deuteronomy. The legislation about what to do with the entrails of the sacrifices, or with fat left over, usually finished me off! Again God used the Boys' Brigade to bring me through. At an enrolment service I was promoted to Corporal and had the privilege of reading a lesson. At the end of the sermon the minister invited people to commit their lives to Christ. To my astonishment one of our officers (Stuart Trotter) went forward. He happened to be my hero at the time, a good footballer as well as chief bugler in the band. He was also beginning on the lay preaching path that was to lead him into the ordained ministry – and *he* needed to give his life to Christ! I was shaken. If *he* needed such commitment, where did *I* stand?

Following that enrolment service a meeting was held at which two local men shared their Christian testimonies. Bill Stoddart, a clerk with the National Coal Board, and Matthew Wigham, a milkman – both of them home from the forces – spoke of their experience of Christ. 'Big Bill' Stoddart, a massive 6' 6" tall, weighing twenty stones and with a voice like a foghorn, was particularly striking, and someone it was difficult to ignore as he thundered: 'I thought I was a big man until I met Jesus!' After their testimonies the minister, Frank Ward, made a further appeal for commitment, and Donald needed no further prodding. The sixteen-year-old walked forward, knelt at the communion rail, and offered his life in Christ's service. The following day Frank Ward cancelled all his meetings and arranged for both Stuart Trotter and Donald English to be at his manse at seven o'clock for follow-up conversations. Donald was there on time, but Stuart was late: his parents ran a butcher's shop and had given him so much work to do after school that he was hard-pressed to get it done in time.

Reflecting on this all-important experience in a *Face to Face* video interview with Lesley Judd many years later, Donald expressed it like this:

> Life was so exciting: I was playing cricket, I was playing football, I was discovering books and reading. I was discovering that there was another sex in the world, and it was all very exciting! But things were very fragmented, and I knew that there was a central thing missing if my life was to have any sort of shape. I remember hearing someone say that he was once given one of those bumper annuals and in the middle there was a double-page spread of a farmyard – a few cows, pigs, ducks and so on. Over the top it said 'Look carefully – what do you see?' At the age of six he felt rather insulted by this; but when he came back later and looked at it again he saw that all those animals and carts and sheds actually made up the head of a lion. It wasn't a farmyard at all: it was a lion's head! That is what happened to me when I gave my life to Christ. All the bits and pieces came together to focus on what I found at the age of sixteen to be a credible lifestyle.[2]

It was not long after this that Donald took his first tentative steps towards local preaching. A Methodist local preacher in Consett named Joe Birch began to take him round the Methodist circuit chapels to help in the leading of worship. That experience formed a significant element in Donald's

---

[2] *Face to Face with Donald English* (Churches' Television Centre).

eventual call to preach – a call that was to be confirmed some years later during his student years in Leicester.

*   *   *   *   *

During his teens Donald was a conscientious boy and spent most evenings working in the small back bedroom. As his next-door neighbour in Leaside, Mrs Gwen Pickersgill (a teacher in the Methodist Sunday school), put it: 'He never went out for anything apart from church and football! He was always studying in his back bedroom – always seemed to be preparing for the future.' Indeed, on one occasion, curious about what motivated him, she asked: 'Donald, you're always studying. What for? Do you want to be a teacher or are you going into the church?' The reply, typical of his later approach to things, but surprisingly mature for a young teenager, was: 'I don't know. I'm praying about it.' Yet he was not so serious as to have no sense of fun: quite the contrary. Gwen Pickersgill recalled how one day, while Donald was studying, her toddler son, David, was making a noise playing in the yard next door. Donald came out and with a twinkle in his eye said: 'I'll keep him quiet!' At that he picked young David up and deposited him in the wash tub outside the back door!

Perhaps his degree of studiousness was unusual, but Donald was in many respects a typical teenager. Another of his friends from those days, Bill Cleasby, describes how large numbers of young people attended the various church youth groups. 'We never got bored in those days', he recalls, 'because we played football whenever we could, often six evenings a week, and then on Sundays we went to church. Most Sunday nights after evening service there would be a youth rally with a speaker at one of our churches, and we would walk in our gangs to wherever the rally was being held.'

Donald was always popular with the girls. He had a number of girlfriends, and was always encouraged to take them home for a cup of tea and some of his favourite coffee cake – often baked especially for him by Mrs Pickersgill in the house next door.

As his faith deepened and matured, Donald began to take the Bible more and more seriously, recognising that it was here that his Christian life would be nurtured. He made daily Bible reading with study notes a part of his spiritual practice, often committing Scripture passages to memory, and gave priority to studying the Bible with other young Christians. At the same time God was clearly preparing him to become a preacher, and he describes one of his earliest experiences in *My Call to Preach*. The incident he recounts happened when he was eighteen years old, not long after he had left Consett to become a student at University College, Leicester. He writes:

A somewhat bizarre incident marked my first extensive presence in a pulpit. I was home on vacation, and when our slightly eccentric Superintendent Minister (Benjamin Drewery) saw me at church one Sunday morning he asked if I was courting. I said I was not, and from this he deduced that I would be free that evening. When I confirmed this he invited me to help him in the conduct of worship. I felt greatly privileged. We met at 5.25pm at the local bus station to travel to a village for a service due to begin at six o'clock. On the bus he suggested that I give out the hymns and do the readings. This seemed fairly hefty for a first commitment in the pulpit, but I agreed. We were interrupted while he paid the fares and then he said, 'I'd like you to take the prayers too, and preach for about fifteen minutes!' It was a quarter to six and the service was due to begin at six.

Donald continues:

When we reached the church he sent me into the pulpit on my own to begin the service, while he returned to the vestry to take off his woolly. I preached for quarter of an hour on a text which stretched from Genesis to Revelation! I included the entire counsel of God, plus a bit more for safety. It was delivered at the speed of an express train, without illustration, application, high or low point. And it was weighty. My colleague then got up and preached for forty minutes. It could hardly have been more different from my offering. The congregation was presented with an unforgettable contrast of style and content that night.

No doubt Donald was being typically over-modest about his own contribution to that service, but even so, these extempore ramblings of a zealous, raw young preacher-in-the-making must have been a far cry from the masterly pulpit skills of his more mature years. Yet every preacher has to begin somewhere, and it was not long before Donald was put 'on note' in his home circuit. This was the first rung on the preaching ladder in the Methodist lay preaching system, and required him always to be accompanied by an accredited preacher. The local preacher Donald was assigned to was none other than Joe Birch, who had already taken him out to help with services several years earlier. Joe took him under his wing and had a considerable influence on Donald's further development as a preacher. Eventually Donald progressed to the next stage as a preacher 'on trial', and was now permitted to take services on his own, though still subject to regular reports on his preaching, made to the Local Preachers' Meeting. Over thirty years later, in April 1986, Donald sent Joe Birch a copy of the book *My Call to Preach*, to which he had contributed, inscribing the title page: 'To Joe and Sarah Birch, with deep gratitude for the part they played in the early days which made one of these chapters possible.'

Donald continued 'on trial' throughout his time at university and most of his subsequent service in the Royal Air Force, finally being fully accredited as a local preacher at the age of twenty-four. The letter of accreditation, dated September 1954, was signed by the then President of the Methodist Conference, Russell Shearer. Donald's Consett friends always looked forward to his returning home for university vacations, or later on leave from the RAF, and he was constantly in demand as a preacher even before he was fully accredited. His friend Bill Cleasby, a fellow preacher, recalled how on one occasion Donald was home on leave and was invited to speak at an open-air meeting in Sherburn Park. He stood up to preach wearing his RAF uniform and took as his text the words 'You must be born again' (John 3:7). By way of introduction he told his audience of an old local preacher he had once heard who spoke on that text every time he preached. When asked why, he simply replied: 'Because that's the most important thing there is – you must be born again!' Although Donald himself could never be accused of being a one-text preacher, the evangelistic challenge of the gospel was always an important element in his preaching.

* * * * *

As we will see in the next chapter, Donald's student years provided him with plenty of opportunity for his Christian commitment to grow and his intellectual grasp of the Christian faith to develop. It was during the two subsequent years of national service, however, that he began to learn how to relate that faith to the secular world. The challenges to his Christian stance in the student world, though real enough, were often in the arena of intellectual debate; life in the RAF was very much more earthy.

Having applied for selection for officer training, Donald was sent in 1953 to the Officer Cadet Training Unit at RAF Spitalgate, near Grantham, Lincolnshire, as one of an intake of about sixty cadets who were being assessed for 'OQs', or 'officer qualities'. He and one of his fellow cadets at that time, Bill Hart, were destined to meet up again many years later when Bill was appointed Principal of Southlands College and while Donald was serving as Chair of the college governors. The officer selection course was a rigorous one, comprising detailed assessment by the Course Commander and his three flight commanders, with further assessment by the RAF Regiment Section on field craft and weapons training. Finally the Education Section put the cadets through a variety of tests, such as public speaking, chairing committee, précis writing and comprehension tests. Quite apart from the rigours of such testing, the challenge of standing firm in his Christian witness was another test that Donald faced head-on. Peter Threlfall, who was a Christian and a fellow officer cadet at Spitalgate, remembers their first night there vividly. 'I said my prayers under the bedclothes', he recalls, 'but Donald without any hesitation knelt down by his bed to pray.'

The Education Officer at Spitalgate in 1953 was John B. Taylor, who later entered the Anglican ministry and eventually became Bishop of St Albans. He recalls Donald's time there in the following terms:

Don came out top of his course and was awarded the Sword of Merit, which meant that apart from being given a certificate and a commemorative plaque, he had to take the passing-out parade as officer-in-charge. This entailed up to three days of drill rehearsals for the full squadron and two supporting squadrons, by which time most Sword of Merit winners would have lost their voices completely before the big day. To the best of my memory Don lasted out – a good sign of his Methodist preacher's lungs and voice control! He was a worthy Sword winner.

Donald qualified as an education officer, initially with the rank of Pilot Officer. He was later promoted to Flying Officer. He was posted to RAF Linton-on-Ouse, near York. Here he became active in the leading of a mid-week Station Church service and fellowship, and is remembered with gratitude by all those who were involved in it, including Derek Mills, now in the Anglican ministry. He writes:

He was a most inspiring preacher and had a great gift for teaching. Many people were indebted to him at Linton for the clarity and patience with which he approached and explained difficult aspects of the faith. It was Don who in 1955 arranged for a party from the Station Church to go to Wembley to hear Billy Graham preach. Without doubt that event changed my life and the ensuing ministry of our padre, Timothy Cook. Don and the fellowship of the church at Linton laid the foundations for my own ministry.

Another Anglican clergyman, Brian Field, recalls how during his student days at St John's College, York, he met a young RAF officer doing his national service:

A few of us students used to meet up with a tutor called Frank Dain and his wife Jean at their home on Sunday afternoons for Bible study. We were joined by some non-students, and one of them was Don English. He had an amazing Bible knowledge for one so young, and was even then very articulate at explaining the faith. Later in life when questioned about this he attributed his knowledge to a course of study produced by the IVF [Inter-Varsity Fellowship, discussed in Chapter 2] called *Search the Scriptures*. It was a three-year course which involved reading the whole Bible and answering (usually in writing) two or three questions each day on the portion read.

However, as on the football field, so too in the RAF camp, there was another side to Donald's character. Derek Mills remembers vividly an occasion when he witnessed Donald 'verbally ripping into an airman because he either had not saluted or had done so in an improper way. Technically, of course, he was right; but the intensity of the attack left a lasting impression on me.' No doubt that one sharp, negative impression was left on his memory in part at least because of the contrast with Donald's normally gracious and friendly manner.

These RAF years provided Donald with a fund of good stories, which later came out in his preaching. John B. Taylor recounts a service he attended at the City Temple, London, for the induction of Janet Sowerbutts as the United Reformed Church Moderator for the North Thames District, at which Donald was the preacher. Also present among the guest clergy was Professor Martin Cressey of Westminster College, Cambridge, who had also been a Spitalgate Sword of Merit winner – as had Bishop Taylor himself. 'Donald, to our slight embarrassment, took the opportunity to remark on this coincidence from the pulpit', writes Bishop Taylor, 'as if to reassure the congregation that whatever our demerits as members of the clergy we had once been very good officer cadets!' Donald added to the occasion by reminiscing of his days at Spitalgate (apocryphally?) in order to illustrate a point, as he was adept at doing. Explaining to the congregation about the drill for falling in on parade, he highlighted the need to have right markers taking up post on the parade ground. Then came the order: 'On your markers, fall in!' The squadron lined up in rows three-deep with the markers on their right. As always, it was a bit of a straggle, so the next command was:

'Right dress!' The ranks did an eyes right, shuffled their feet to make the rows straight and lined up before the order: 'Eyes front!' Donald explained that most of the cadets had come straight from university, so were better at other things than drill. When the Warrant Officer saw that the rows continued to shuffle, he spotted that the right markers were not standing firm. The air was blue for a while. The college rookies soon learned that order came when the markers stood firm. Donald's point, of course, was that the church would be forever wavering unless it had a firm and immovable point of reference.

Although life in both Leicester and Linton had extended his horizons, Donald was always glad to return to Consett to spend time with his parents and to renew the friendships of his early days. His affection for his roots remained strong throughout his life, and it was always both a great joy for him and a proud moment for Consett whenever he returned 'home' in the subsequent years of his ministry. His passion for the north-east was clearly evidenced too by his lifelong support for Newcastle United – a passion shared by the late Cardinal Basil Hume. During Donald's second term as President of the Methodist Conference a Newcastle newspaper carried the headline 'Magpie Faithfuls' and reported:

> Britain's top churchmen may be on different teams when it comes to religion – but they are *United* on football. Roman Catholic leader Cardinal Basil Hume and his Methodist counterpart, Reverend Dr Donald English, are confirmed Magpie fans. The pair are well acquainted and closely follow the team's changing fortunes. 'We commiserate with one another and congratulate one another on their results, and Newcastle usually features in the letters we write to one another,' said Dr English.

Letters from Cardinal Hume illustrate the point. On 5 January 1987 Basil Hume wrote to Donald: 'I am in total despair about Newcastle. I even now believe that it would be worse to be a Director of Newcastle United than to be Archbishop of Westminster! I never thought I would live to come to that conclusion.' Three months later, on 9 April 1987, Hume wrote: 'I think that we might just miss relegation. If we do go down you and I might have to examine the quality of our prayer!'

In the summer of 1977, after the Methodist Conference had voted Donald as President-Designate for the first time, his parents received a letter from the then Chair of the Newcastle upon Tyne District, Wesley Earl, expressing the delight of the District: 'I know that you will both be excited at the prospect and the whole District rejoices with you. It has voted for Donald steadily through recent years as he has gone up the list, and in a very real sense I feel that he will be *their* President.' The following year, as his induction approached, Donald received a letter from Joe Birch, the local preacher who had been of such help to him as he first began preaching, offering prayers and good wishes for his year of office. Joe Birch wrote:

> Memory goes back over the years and I recall with joy your first service one Sunday morning with me at Blackhill Durham Road Church – must be about 30 years ago! I had great hopes for you after that service and have prayed and watched with spiritual interest your dedicated service for God and his Kingdom, but beyond my wildest dreams that he would so graciously lead you to this high office of leadership. I believe he has much to say through you.

On a visit to the Newcastle District during his second presidency in 1991 Donald was talking about Consett to the then Bishop of Durham, David Jenkins, who offered to lend him a book on the social history of the town, a community with equally strong Roman Catholic and Nonconformist traditions. Donald's letter when returning the book some months later reveals something of his feeling for his roots in Consett Methodism:

> You can imagine how saddened I was by the story, first because it confirmed the way in which people of that area trusted those in authority only to be let down again and again. You have probably seen the musical *Close the Coal House Door* by Alex Douglas. I watched it on television and simply sat and wept after it. It was like looking at an X-ray of the life of the town in which I grew up. But I am also saddened by the uneven presentation in the book itself. It tends to give the impression that you are not socially concerned if you're not both Roman Catholic and adept at the use of bad language! I have to say that the Consett it describes is one I am wholly unfamiliar with. I am amazed that there is no mention of people from the Methodist side who did such an enormous amount for the conditions of the workers and struggled to improve the overall situation. A man like Charlie Stirling, who was leader of the Boilermakers' Union and a Methodist Local Preacher, should surely have been mentioned. Then there was Alan Marshall, another staunch Methodist, who was chosen from the workers' side to be a director of a Consett Iron Company. Thank you for sending the book to me. It made painful reading but, as you can tell, it also stirred me up!

*   *   *   *   *

Many years before Donald's rise to such national prominence, soon after his graduation from University College, Leicester, the local Consett newspaper had carried a report under the heading 'Young Man of Promise'. It read:

> A local young man coming well to the fore in religious and public speaking activities is Mr Donald English, BA, a product

of our local Council and Grammar Schools. The town is proud of such young leaders and looks with confidence to its future with such men of character directing its life.

Little did anyone know at that time what that future really held.

2

Student Work

In 1948, at the age of eighteen, Donald became a student at
what was then University College, Leicester.[1] As an under-
graduate, Donald read history, a subject to which he continued throughout his life to attach great importance. On his
arrival in Leicester, Donald soon linked up with two Methodist churches, Frederick Street Methodist Church, South
Wigston, the area where he was living, and Clarendon Park
Methodist Church (now Trinity), a flourishing church of
about three hundred near the university. The congregation
included a large body of students. It was here that Donald
met Bertha Ludlow, his future wife. At Clarendon Park,
after Sunday evening worship, an 'at home hour' was
hosted by the church, and many students came, including
Donald. There would be a speaker or some special event.
Donald was also drawn to evangelistic open-air meetings in
Leicester that were held on Sunday evenings, and one day he
found himself being told that he was next to speak at one
of these. As we have seen, he already had preaching experience. He became part of the student preaching team that
went into the Leicester south circuit, encouraged by three

---

[1] For his days as a student see A. Warrell, 'Donald English – Student' in R.W. Abbott (ed.), *Donald English: An Evangelical Cele-*
bration (Ilkeston, Derbyshire: Headline Special/Moorleys, 1999),
pp. 8–13. Parts of this chapter are indebted to Warrell's chapter.

Methodist ministers: Sydney Gordon, Ronald E. South and Willoughby Thompson. The students mainly went to village chapels.

One person who came to faith through Donald's preaching at one of the open-air meetings held in Leicester market was John Bedford. He became a Methodist minister, but subsequently joined the Baptist denomination and became deeply involved in the charismatic movement, moving into wider itinerant ministry in the 1980s. John Bedford describes how he was wandering through Leicester city market-place one winter evening on his way to the cinema to see the film *Gone with the Wind*. His attention was arrested by a group that was singing and giving Christian testimony. He was struck by the preaching of a 'redhead' leader, who turned out to be Donald English. John Bedford stopped to listen and argue – and missed the film. As he came to know Donald, Bedford was impressed by the maturity, wisdom and forthright commitment to Jesus Christ that he saw in him. Bedford went for several weeks to the open-air meetings, read John's Gospel, and committed his life to Christ as his Saviour at a Sunday evening service in Melbourne Hall, Leicester, in May 1951. The role of Donald English had been crucial.

A very important part of Donald's life at university was the college Christian Union (CU), which was a part of the conservative evangelical Inter-Varsity Fellowship of Evangelical Unions (IVF), formed in 1928. It was through this group perhaps more than any other connection that his personal faith deepened. Evangelicalism, with its emphasis on personal conversion, active mission, the authority of the Bible and the centrality of the cross of Christ,[2] experienced a resurgence in the post-war period. The IVF was a key

---

[2] D.W. Bebbington, *Evangelicalism in Modern Britain: A History from the 1730s to the 1980s* (London: Routledge, 1995), pp. 2–17.

element in this process. When Donald arrived at university
the CU had existed for only one year and was still small. The
photos of the CU taken annually indicate the growth that
was then happening and which was in line with the expan-
sion in IVF work that was taking place in all British universities.[3] In 1948 there were nine members in the photo; in
1950, seventeen, including Donald; and in 1951, thirty-
seven.[4] Attendance could be up to seventy. Donald's gifts
were soon recognised by the CU committee. At an early
stage he became 'Publications Secretary', that is, book steward. He also became CU President, serving from 1951 to
1952. The Publications Secretary had outreach opportunities, which Donald relished. As well as looking after a selection of books useful for CU members, he sold books at open
meetings. There was also a book table set up in the college
crush hall once a week. It was through this that contact was
made with other students. A college of 700 undergraduates
was a fairly tightly knit community. Donald, with two other
CU members, George Measures and Tony Davis, organised
'freshers' socials' and end of term entertainment with
great success.

Donald Grundy recalls his experience as a fresher coming
to Leicester, and of attending one of the freshers' socials,
held at the corn exchange. Three students who were not
freshers suddenly burst on to the stage and completely
disrupted the proceedings, much to the amusement of
Grundy and the other freshers present. The three students
interrupted practically every programmed item presented
by the Students' Union (which had planned the event), but
no one seemed to mind. Their 'turn' was slapstick, but it

---

[3] D. Johnson, *Contending for the Faith: A History of the Evangelical Movement in the Universities and Colleges* (Leicester:
IVP, 1979), p. 235.

[4] G. Fielder, *Lord of the Years: Sixty Years of Student Witness*
(Leicester: IVP, 1988), p. 136.

was 'quality' slapstick, highly amusing and very appropriate to the occasion. For Grundy there was one 'fool', Donald English, who stood out as the prince of fools. They seemed such natural clowns that it was difficult to believe on that evening that they had any other role to play in university life. Grundy and others discovered that Donald had indeed a great sense of humour and an appreciation of the zany side of life. He was known on at least one occasion to sell second-hand clothes in Leicester market. Those who did not witness his humour elsewhere soon discovered it in his sermons and talks, when the timing of his humour – with invariably a clearly recognisable link with the theme of his address – was greatly appreciated by the whole congregation or audience.

Grundy was already a Methodist and Donald English duly introduced him to the CU. They were also fellow worshippers at Clarendon Park Methodist Church. Oliver Barclay (who was General Secretary of the IVF from 1964 to 1980), in his *Evangelicalism in Britain, 1935–1995*, comments that in terms of the Christian scene in universities in this period the theologically mixed Student Christian Movement (SCM) began to falter, though it still had much official support. It was further weakened by the growth of denominational societies, particularly the Methodist societies.[5] From the perspective of Peter Richards, a Methodist who was in the Leicester SCM at the same time as Donald English was in the CU, everything that the CU organised was deliberately planned to clash with the SCM. Christianity became, Richards comments, a big laughing stock in the college. Who, people asked, were the Christians? Was it the SCM-ites or the CU-ites? The CU members were seen by the SCM members as looking down upon them and regarding them as second-class

[5] O. Barclay, *Evangelicalism in Britain, 1935–1995* (Leicester: IVP, 1997), pp. 65–6.

Christians. Later Donald would bring to his evangelicalism a much broader outlook and would be ready, as Richards wished, to appreciate those with different Christian experiences.

In the 1950s, however, the views of the CU members were shaped by the wider religious background of the time. Oliver Barclay describes how the movement grew in the 1950s but how in this period many conservative evangelicals 'felt themselves to be a rather despised minority in their churches' and had often been told by others that to be a conservative evangelical in approaching the Bible meant 'they had to run away from the theological problems or become obscurantist'.[6] Geraint Fielder, in his book *Lord of the Years*, quotes Donald English regarding the 1950s. It was a period when 'we evangelicals were very much more in the situation of fighting with our backs to the wall', recalled Donald:

> The 'fundamentalist witch-hunt' was on. We had very few established evangelical scholars then. Those we had, like Alan Stibbs and the young Jim Packer, were also expected to spend their days travelling the country, speaking at meetings ... The theological scene was almost totally alien to us, apart from the evangelical Anglican colleges. I think our sense of having to defend what was under severe attack probably widened the gap between us and other Christians in order to ensure clarity about our own position. And we may, in our suspicion of the social gospel, have neglected social and political issues. On the other hand, we were quite clear that we were really in the business of bringing spiritual babes to birth and then handling them in the earlier stages of their lives ... I cannot thank God enough for what I learned through IVF.[7]

---

[6] Ibid. pp. 70, 72.
[7] Fielder, *Lord of the Years*, pp. 178–9.

This last statement illustrates the committed evangelist in Donald. Much of his work was with individuals and he led several to Christian commitment. He also, however, saw the mission potential of larger events. On one occasion he was able to engage in a public university debate in defence of the Christian faith. Donald's public speaking and debating skills were already becoming evident. At this Students' Union debate he opposed the motion put by Bryan Wilson, who later became a Fellow of All Souls, Oxford, and a distinguished writer on the sociology of religion. The proposition put forward was that 'This House does not believe in an Afterlife'. The debate, says Alan Warrell, caught the interest of the whole college, and while Donald spoke the CU members were praying for him to be persuasive. Donald made what was recognised to be an outstanding speech and the motion was defeated. It was through his CU involvement that Donald's own understanding of the Christian faith deepened and became more informed. He was never to move from the evangelical beliefs of this period.

Donald was also to remain faithful to his early Methodist convictions. While at Leicester he made his presence felt in the local Methodist scene, not just by his speaking, but also by his personality. John and Margaret Hilton, who were teenagers in the Frederick Street Methodist Church, recall the sense of the 'tremendous vitality' of Donald English when he attended their services. At what was called the 'monthly special' at Clarendon Park Church, Donald heard some of the most prominent Methodists in the country preach. Wilbert Howard, Principal of Handsworth College, Ernest Rattenbury, who had preached at the church when it first opened in 1900 and had done so every year since that time, and Eric Waterhouse, Principal of Richmond College, came each year to Clarendon Park. Other leading Methodist speakers included the theologian Newton Flew and preachers such as W.E. Sangster and Howard Watkin Jones. Donald, like others, was introduced to the world of Methodist theology and Methodist preaching. From an early stage Donald had an awareness of the tensions between different theological positions. The books in his extensive library reflected the breadth of his studies. As a small indication of his desire to identify both with inter-denominational evangelicalism and with Methodism he used to wear a Scripture Union badge in one lapel and an MAYC (Methodist Association of Youth Clubs) badge in the other. He was a Methodist, but was more than a Methodist.

Christian activity was not something that Donald allowed to divert him from his academic work, although competing priorities were a struggle. He was committed to achieving a good standard in his degree studies at Leicester. Professor Simmonds, Head of the Department of History, was a noted historian and an interesting lecturer, and Donald made steady progress with his studies. A friend from that period, Tony Davis, recalls that Donald was annoying as a fellow student, since while others toiled away, Donald would switch on only at the last moment, and would cope with everything set in examinations. He gained a University of London BA, second class, upper division, after three years. External first-class honours degrees from the University of London were very rare. Two contemporaries of Donald, Bryan Wilson and Alan Walters, who became an adviser to Margaret Thatcher, were exceptions. After gaining his BA Donald entered the Department of Education and in 1953 gained a credit in his PGCE (Postgraduate Certificate of Education), one of only two students to obtain that level of distinction in that year. Donald would have been a fine schoolteacher, and his practical training in this field, through teaching practice in local schools, would contribute to his ability as a communicator. Subsequently, in 1994, the University of Leicester would honour him with an honorary DLitt (Doctor of Letters).

One theme that was taken up by the Public Orator, Professor W. Forster, on the occasion of the award of the DLitt to Donald English was Donald's acknowledged sporting prowess. Donald was a fine cricketer and was an outstanding footballer, whose skills meant that he could have made football his career. He was already on Sunderland's books as an amateur, and he also went on to Leicester City's books. Approaches from Wolves were rejected, as this would have interfered with his appearances for the college and for the English and British universities' sides. He also played for the Universities' Athletic Union. In the college team he played as right back and captain. He declined a trial for the England International Amateur Football Team as the event was on a Sunday. The oration by Professor Forster left the audience in no doubt about the importance of sport for Donald: 'During the summer months, he restricted himself to playing cricket for the College and, maybe between overs or during wet spells, read enough to take a degree in History. He then bought himself another season by taking a Diploma in Education.'[8] Donald Grundy, who played with Donald English in the same University College cricket team, recalls that on occasions he captained the side, and that all respected his fairness, able leadership and gentlemanly behaviour on the field.

The spirit in which Donald played was, for Grundy, an instance of his Christian example. Alan Boulton, as a fellow sportsman, confirms the way in which Donald held together his passion for sport and his commitment to witnessing for Christ. Boulton wrote:

One of my treasured possessions is a membership card for the Christian Union at Leicester. It is dated 29th October 1951 and it is signed Don English. My joining the Union came about

---

[8] University of Leicester, 'Congregation for the Conferment of Honorary Degrees', 10 November 1994.

because I was a football referee, joined the football club and did a mixture of refereeing and acting as linesman. Donald's manner of life impressed me for he had something I lacked and this was something I wanted.

B.W. Hearn, another student, was, as he put it, 'naïve enough to be surprised that an enthusiastic Christian could be a classy footballer'. It was football that drew him to talk to Donald, and Donald led him to Christian commitment. Alan Boulton was a member of the university football team that went on a tour to Germany in 1951. Donald was the captain. One outstanding memory of this tour is that the team members received a very warm welcome from German people. Sport was helping to highlight the possibility of post-war reconciliation; the theme of reconciliation was one to which Donald attached great importance.

Christian Union involvement remained central for Donald during the whole of his period at Leicester. Alan Warrell recalls that when an Inter-Varsity mission to the university was proposed it was Donald, who was soon to take his finals, who was the obvious choice for Mission Committee Chair. The IVF was seeking to take advantage of what was a time of openness among many university students to Christian apologetic, and missions were being held in a number of universities and colleges. The Revd the Hon. Roland Lamb was invited to be the main missioner in Leicester. Roland Lamb was then a Methodist minister and at that time was also an IVF travelling secretary. Later he became the General Secretary of the British Evangelical Council and operated largely outside Methodism. Lamb was to have an impact in Leicester – one that influenced many students. His regular visits to the colleges introduced Methodists to the Revival Fellowship which had been formed in Methodism and of which Lamb was one of the leaders. Donald became and remained an active member of

the Methodist Revival Fellowship (MRF). Of great significance was the number of students in Leicester who subsequently offered themselves for the Christian ministry. Six
became Methodist ministers and many others dedicated
themselves to home and overseas service.

A group from the Leicester CU joined the IVF camp at the
Keswick Convention in 1953. The Convention was (and is)
a large annual gathering of evangelicals held in the Lake
District town of that name. The distinctive teaching of the
Keswick meetings, from their inception in 1875, is that the
Christian is called to a life of holiness, in the sense of victory
over sin, and that this life is entered into by full surrender to
Christ. Donald spent some sleepless hours wrestling with
this 'holiness' teaching and with what was sometimes called
'The Second Blessing'. Although Keswick's emphasis was a
variant of John Wesley's understanding of the possibility of
'Christian Perfection', such thinking about the Christian
life was not prevalent in Methodism in the 1950s. Donald
would never become an advocate of a particular approach
to holiness, but he was to call on Methodists to take
seriously John Wesley's belief that (as Donald put it in his
presidential address to the Methodist Conference in 1990)
'the love of God could so control the centre of the believer's
being that every thought, attitude, word and deed could
issue from this fountain of divine love at the centre of one's
life'. We neglect this 'fundamental part of Methodist spirituality', Donald warned, 'at our peril'. Later, as we will see,
Donald would be a valued speaker on the Keswick Convention platform. Keswick has traditionally not had many
Methodist speakers and therefore the presence of Donald
was significant.

Those who knew Donald in this period speak of his spiritual insight and his profound understanding of the Bible.
He was also very thorough in various types of committee
work. In individual conversation he had a remarkable way

of giving another person his whole attention and of being sensitive to the need to pray with someone. It is not surprising that the world of the IVF saw his potential. For his part, Donald had a vision of Christians, especially evangelical Christians, working together. There were other colleges in Leicester and with some members of the CU Donald brought about the Leicester Inter-Collegiate Christian Union (LICCU), linking University College with the domestic science college, the teacher training college, the technical college and the speech therapy college. There was a wider gathering of Midland colleges Christian Unions and in 1952 Donald became the Midland representative on the Executive Committee of the IVF. He became responsible for organising the termly conferences. In 1953 he was involved in a Leicester CU mission in West Ham, London. His debt to the CU and to the wider IVF movement was one he was glad to acknowledge.

One conversation in which Donald Grundy was involved in 1953 indicates the way in which the calibre of Donald English could be discerned at that early stage by those who knew him well. Grundy was asked a question by a fellow student when three or four students were talking together. The results of the Postgraduate Certificate of Education had just been published. Fifty years on, Grundy remembers the precise wording of the question and of his answer. 'Will Don continue in teaching after receiving that grade?' Grundy's answer was: 'He may teach for a while but even that cannot be certain. Before long he will enter the Methodist ministry and one day will become President of Conference.' The questioner, understandably, replied: 'You can't be serious.' 'I could not be more serious', Grundy replied with remarkable confidence. 'Just wait and see. Time will prove me correct.' Others saw the same kind of potential. When Grundy wrote to Donald to congratulate him on his appointment as President of the Methodist

Conference in 1979 he mentioned this conversation. Grundy did not realise that his prophecy, made in the light of his association with Donald English over a period of four years, would prove to be only half-correct, since Donald became President twice.

*   *   *   *   *

After completing his degree at Leicester, as we have seen, Donald went on to do two years of national service in the RAF. He continued to play football, often being flown to his matches, and completed his Methodist local preacher training. He was then invited to become a travelling secretary for the IVF, covering the Midlands and the north of England. This job, which he held from 1955 to 1958, meant a great deal of travelling and speaking at university and college CU meetings, conferences and missions, and he exercised a significant ministry both as an evangelist and in encouraging others to be active in evangelism. People were converted to Christ both through his public speaking and his personal conversations. One example was a student at Loughborough College, John Young (who was later to become a Canon of York Minster and a popular author), who was converted largely through Donald's ministry. John Young was invited to a CU weekend at which Donald, as an IVF travelling secretary, was speaking, and Young was made to think deeply by what he heard. During some free time Donald invited him to go for a walk and a chat, and both the substance of that conversation and Donald's willingness to give his free time to a student whom he did not know made a deep impression on John Young. That weekend became a turning point for him and soon afterwards he became a committed Christian.

It would be wrong to think that Donald English took on responsibilities as a speaker without them causing him any anxieties. He related at the Keswick Convention in 1993 an occasion during his IVF ministry when he was invited to the Leeds University CU to give a talk entitled 'The Impossibility of Agnosticism'. The talk had been advertised without Donald being consulted about the title, and he protested to the CU's committee that it was an inappropriate title, since clearly agnosticism could not be impossible – it existed. Nothing could be done about this, as the talk had been widely advertised, so Donald went to the meeting feeling that 'my tongue was cleaving to the roof of my mouth'. The lecture hall was completely full and the Chair, a student, pointed out to Donald that the entire committee of the Communist Party was present and that even the Professor of Spanish, the best-known atheist in the university, had come along. Donald did his best and after speaking he asked for questions. The first question was from the Professor of Spanish, who said that he thought that he had been about to hear a lecture on radiation (he had come to the wrong lecture), but he proceeded to ask a question which gave Donald exactly the opportunity he needed to emphasise his own argument.

John C. Newton, who was a student in Southampton, describes an IVF mission that took place there in September 1955, just as Donald was starting work with the IVF. This was an annual summer mission, and in 1955 there was a widespread take-up from the churches, with about eighteen or nineteen involved. The Billy Graham Crusade in Harringay had been held in the previous year and there was great interest in evangelism. At least two of the churches that were participating in the local mission were Methodist. John and Pam Newton were allocated to the team at Northam Methodist Church. Sidney Lawrence, who was one of the founders of the MRF, was the leader of this team, Donald was assistant leader, and Rosina Parker of London Bible College was the women's leader. Geoffrey Ainger was minister of the church. Northam was a small, inner-city congregation, set in dense Victorian working-class housing. Geoffrey Ainger, says Newton, might have been seen as an unlikely person to welcome an IVF team, given the IVF's strong conservative evangelical stance, but he had a genuine concern for mission.

The main tensions that emerged in this mission were not, in fact, because IVF members were working with a Methodist church that would not have been regarded as conservative in its theology. Instead, the difficulties arose because of Arminian-Calvinist differences within the team. Sidney Lawrence had strong Calvinistic beliefs. He later left Methodism. His worries about 'easy believism' meant that he did not believe in any open appeals to people to respond publicly to the messages. Throughout the week, therefore, no appeals of this kind were made. After the Friday of the mission week, Sidney Lawrence had to return to Methodist circuit duties, and Donald took over the leadership of the team. On the final Sunday evening of the mission a congregation of about 100 assembled, which filled the church and which represented almost twice the church membership. Donald gave a powerful message, made an appeal (which was a normal way of operating for him), and thirteen people responded. In those days and in that setting, John Newton comments, such a level of response was justifiably regarded as something of a miracle.

These Arminian-Calvinist tensions are illustrative of the internal doctrinal issues that the IVF had to face. Under its General Secretary at the time, Douglas Johnson, the IVF sought to deal with these kinds of issues when it brought IVF staff workers together at staff conferences. For example, in November 1955 Johnson wrote to the IVF staff members, including Donald, outlining the different views held among evangelicals about the Second Advent and recommending books to be read in preparation for the 1956

staff conference when the topic would be studied.[9] The
IVF leadership saw the need to prevent evangelicals from
dividing over secondary issues. There were attacks by many
church leaders on evangelicals and on 'fundamentalism',
climaxing in strong opposition to Billy Graham's Cambridge University mission of 1955. Some British Christian
leaders feared that a wave of obscurantist evangelicalism of
the fundamentalist type was about to engulf Western Christianity. In February 1956 Michael Ramsey, then Bishop of
Durham and soon to become Archbishop of York, made
rather vague charges in the Durham diocesan magazine,
The Bishoprick, about Billy Graham having taught un-
acceptable doctrines at his recent mission in Cambridge.

Donald's schedule in the period 1955 to 1958 was a
heavy one. The autumn term of 1957, for example, saw him
in Sheffield, Hull, Birmingham, Dublin, Belfast, Leicester,
Loughborough, Leeds, Bradford, Wakefield, Manchester,
Newcastle, Consett and Liverpool, speaking at a wide variety of mainly student events. As his initial appointment with
the IVF came to its close, he was asked if he would stay on
for a further year or two. His acceptance within the IVF is
evidenced by the fact that he led the Bible studies for the
IVF staff conference in June 1958. Donald was, however,
already coming to the belief that his future direction was in
the Methodist ministry. On 16 April 1958 he wrote in one
of his regular prayer letters to his friends that he was
approaching his final term as a travelling secretary and
that he would be becoming a theological student. He
commented that: 'The way won't be too easy, so if you can
retain some small corner on your list for one theological
student, I'd be most grateful!' As well as the sense of call to
ordained ministry, he felt that to go on dealing with the
same questions about Christian faith and practice that

---

[9] Letter No. 3 from Douglas Johnson, November 1955.

successive years of students raised with him would possibly make him too repetitive and stale.

Describing his call to Methodist ministry at a meeting in Belfast in 1993, Donald pinpointed a holiday during his time as a travelling secretary, which turned out to be decisive. All those on the holiday were single professional people. A conversation developed over coffee in which some of the others asked Donald what he thought he would do in the future. He replied that he was considering the ordained ministry, and one of the young women who was in the group said: 'I think you'd have a lot to offer in the ministry.' The young woman was Bertha, his future wife. What would he offer? During his time with the IVF Donald had become increasingly convinced of the importance of biblical exposition. This was one primary commitment that he would take with him into ministry. To those who asked him about the secret of his ability to explain the Bible in such a compelling way he might speak of methods of preaching, as we will see in Chapter 7, but he would also indicate that there was, at the root of preaching, a desire to draw from the Bible for oneself. The IVF helped him to nurture this desire and was among the important background influences that shaped him on his way to ordained ministry.

It was during his later period as a travelling secretary that Donald began the Methodist ministerial candidating process, and in 1958, having passed the various examinations, he appeared before the 'July' Committee. Alan Warrell suggests that the committee gave him a rough passage, particularly over his adherence to the doctrine of substitutionary atonement. The committee no doubt found itself in an unusual position, interviewing someone so thoroughly immersed in the world of inter-denominational conservative evangelical thought. However, Conference accepted him, and in September 1958 Donald entered Wesley House,

Cambridge. Two years were spent at Cambridge studying for the tripos part II under such well-known ministers and theological teachers as W.F. Flemington, Philip Watson, Michael Skinner and Owen Chadwick. Donald applied himself in a disciplined way to his studies, including the study of the Greek New Testament. He mastered the Greek language so well that the Wesley House Principal, W.F. Flemington, asked Donald to help by tutoring some of the slow learners. Being older and more experienced than some of the other housemen, and with his irrepressible sense of humour, Don played a leading role in the life of the house and in due course became Chair.

As always, Donald had other interests. He played football, naturally, and each Wednesday afternoon a training session was held on Jesus Green, Cambridge, under Donald's leadership. He was captain of the house team. Donald and two others from the house played with the Fitzwilliam team, Wesley House and Fitzwilliam House being affiliated, and this team won the Cambridge Inter-College Cup, a feat never accomplished before. A special dinner was given in honour of the three housemen. It was during this time, however, that Donald began to suffer with his back, a problem that would recur throughout his life. His other main interest was in Christian societies in the house and the university. Three times a week at the end of the day the MRF members in the house met for prayer. He also played his part in a MethSoc (Methodist student society) group. This, together with his membership of CICCU (Cambridge Inter-Collegiate Christian Union), gave him wider contacts in the university. Donald's contact with John Stott, later Rector of All Souls Church, Langham Place, which began when he was a travelling secretary, led to the establishment of summer house parties at John Stott's home, The Hookses, on the coast of Pembrokeshire, for ex-Leicester friends and others. Donald led these events.

While at Wesley House he also co-operated with Howard Marshall – later Professor Howard Marshall, the distinguished Methodist New Testament scholar – in the production of *Christian Beliefs* for Inter-Varsity Press (IVP). In 1960 Donald sat the Cambridge Tripos and was awarded an upper-second class degree.

* * * * *

Student life for Donald was now at an end. His interest in students would, however, continue throughout his career, and Chapter 5 will look at his role as a theological teacher. He also continued to have a great interest in lay people who wished to study. In the early 1990s, for example, he was aware of the impact that the *DISCIPLE* Bible study programme was having on churches in the USA and he brought about the establishment of a Methodist steering group to examine how this material could be adapted and used in the UK. The material was launched in the UK at Westminster Central Hall in 1996. Linda Hernandez, the co-ordinator of the scheme, has noted that as a result of participating in groups related to the study programme ten people have felt called to offer themselves to train as ordained ministers, thirty-one have felt led to train as Methodist local preachers and others have taken up lay ministries. Donald's enthusiasm for this type of training in the 1990s shows that his concern for students, which dated back to 1948, remained unabated. 'I hope', he said as IVF travelling secretary to his prayer supporters in 1958, 'you will feel it right to continue to pray for Student Work.'[10] Donald English's IVF connections significantly shaped his vision for ministry. That vision, which drew also upon John Wesley's belief that the world was his parish, was no

---

[10] D. English prayer letter, 16 April 1958.

narrow or limited one. Rather, it embraced a world-wide view of ministry, and one which was soon to see him offering for service overseas.

3

Missionary Service

The archive note now filed in the World Church Office of the Methodist Church in London and dated November 1965 is brief and to the point. It simply records:

> Rev Donald English BA first went to Africa in 1962, and served as Methodist tutor at Trinity College in Umuahia, Eastern Nigeria. This is a joint theological training college for Presbyterian, Anglican and Methodist ministers. Mr English, with his wife and their sons Richard and Paul, returned to England in January 1966 to take up the Home Work.

1962 was a very significant year for Donald English in more ways than one. Not only did he sail to West Africa to begin a term of four years' missionary work in Nigeria, but before that he was ordained at the Methodist Conference held in Stoke-on-Trent, and was married to his fiancée, Bertha Ludlow. Bertha was a graduate of Birmingham University (Theology, French and English) with a subsequent London Postgraduate Diploma in Education. She had been senior mistress at Coalville Grammar School, appointed at the remarkably early age of twenty-five, and then became Lady Warden of McArthur Hall at the Methodist College, Belfast. Her family was well known in Irish Methodism and also overseas, and no less than seven members of the family of

Bertha's generation married ministers of various denominations. Donald and Bertha's wedding was conducted by one of her uncles, D. Hall Ludlow, and the best man was Laurie Churms, a Methodist minister who had been a close friend of Donald's during their student days together in Leicester. As family commitments allowed, Bertha would later continue her teaching career, but for now she saw her primary role as being to work in partnership with Donald in his ministry – and this she did superbly well.

There were those in British Methodism at that time who questioned whether going overseas was the best use of Donald English's undoubted gifts. In particular, his fellow evangelicals knew that there were few people of his calibre or ability in their ranks, and some felt that he should have remained at home and exerted his influence within British Methodism. The passage of time showed them to be too hasty in their judgement and too impatient in their desires. Donald himself had absolutely no doubt that he was obeying a clear call from God. Over a decade later, when addressing a missionary meeting during the 1974 Derwent Convention at Cliff College, he put it like this:

> Let me disabuse you of the idea that being a missionary is something irresistibly glamorous. When we talk about going to serve God overseas we're not talking about exciting, romantic things. We're talking about the way of obedience. And when we talk about becoming a missionary we're not talking about some magical change that takes place when you're on the ship or the plane. Whatever your weaknesses are in this country they will be magnified over there.

It is clear from the way he continued his address at Cliff College that for Donald the tremendous physical and spiritual needs he saw in Africa and the challenge to respond to them were major factors in his own call. He continued:

Many of us are still haunted by Francis Glendinning's illustration: If you started a queue of starving people at the door of your home tonight and let them queue around the circumference of the world (let us say 25,000 miles), it would still pass your door again as the queue formed – and again and again. It would pass the door 25 times! ... Or did you know that there are about 700 million illiterate adults in the world and that number is added to by between 20,000 and 25,000 every year? ... And did you know that there are well over 14 million refugees in the world and that number is growing all the time? Does that look to you like the world that the Creator intended? It is not only horrific; it's blasphemous ... You may say, of course, that there is great need in England. Aren't other countries sending missionaries to us? Yes, they are – but there is one very subtle difference. The missionaries in this country are so close together that you can hardly move for them compared with what you find overseas. You go out to parts of Asia and Africa and you'll find that one minister is looking after 90 churches, 12 schools and 2 hospitals. Does that seem right to you, my brothers and sisters?[1]

What Donald expressed in such vivid and challenging terms at the Derwent Convention he had put rather differently back in January 1961 when completing the Candidates' Application Form for overseas service with what was then the Methodist Missionary Society. Scribbling the words 'Brief and hasty!' at the top of the page, his answer to a question about the missionary obligation of the church gives an interesting insight into how he understood his call and the nature of the missionary task to which he was committing himself:

1. In obedience to our Lord's command we must preach the gospel to every nation. This will involve proclamation,

---

[1] Cliff College Recordings, Derwent Convention, 1974.

with care about local thought-forms and background; and apologetic, in view of the challenge of non-Christian religions.

2. Because of the ethical implications of the gospel we must also seek to improve the social conditions of under-developed countries, and to supply whatever material aid is needed.

3. The establishing of local churches will follow from the proclamation of the gospel, and these must be instructed and led increasingly to responsible autonomy by gradual stages, playing their part in a family of brother and sister churches rather than prolonging the mother–daughter relationship.

4. The interpretation of the gospel in terms of local situation will also be necessary, lest the gospel be seen as an 'optional extra' in areas where the claims and pretensions of politics seem to be all-embracing.

A further question in that same application form asked candidates to say what contribution they believed they would be able to make to the church overseas. Donald wrote:

1. The specific task involved in the post suggested (theological college tutor) is that of theological training, and one's chief concern will be to provide an adequate basis theologically and spiritually to support a successful and sustained ministry.

2. One would hope too to provide help in preaching and pastoralia, as well as making one's own preaching and pastoral contribution.

3. In the setting of a Union college one would hope to further the right kind of inter-denominational relationships.

4. My fiancée and I are praying that as man and wife we may be enabled to make a contribution along the lines of establishing a truly Christian home life.

5. I have a certain amount of experience in youth work and evangelism, and would be glad to be involved in these spheres if possible.

Those answers were clearly satisfactory to the Society and so it was that, as the climax to an eventful year, Donald and Bertha set sail as newly-weds for West Africa. Those were the days before missionaries were flown to their assignments, and the long voyage provided a welcome respite from the stresses and pressures of the previous few months. Donald and Bertha were able to relax on board and enjoy the company of each other. Several years later, when giving a series of Bible readings on the First Epistle of Peter at the Keswick Convention, Donald recalled that experience and turned it, in his own inimitable way, into an effective illustration: 'We would often stand on deck at night and see the moon, its light reflected in a line across the ocean right to where we were. It was a great temptation to dive in and try to swim to the moon! And every time you meet a new convert, there's a line right back into the very being of God.' Donald's application from Peter was: 'Peter says when you came to Christ you started in the foreknowledge of God.'

*   *   *   *   *

The Englishes' destination, Umuahia, was a good-sized town situated in the region that stretched east of the Niger to the Cameroon boundary and from the Berue River in the north to the coast of the Gulf of Biafra. It was the main regional centre for the area. In addition to Trinity Theological College, the Queen Elizabeth Hospital was situated there. Eileen Wragg, another British missionary, had preceded Donald and Bertha and was already working at the Lay Training Centre on the other side of the township when they arrived. She writes:

Soon after they came to Umuahia, I invited them to dinner. Bertha had been welcomed by all the insects in the area, and her arms and legs were covered in blisters. I was able to comfort her by saying that the same thing had happened to me at the beginning of my first tour! We had coconut cream for dessert, made of course from fresh coconut. Years later, when I met Don back in England, he referred again to 'that delicious sweet we ate together in Umuahia'.

Donald and Bertha lived on the college campus, an idyllic hilltop setting a couple of miles or so out of town. Their home was a bungalow with rendered block walls and a corrugated iron roof, and the windows had the customary wire mesh covers to keep the mosquitoes out, and shutters which were closed at night. The kitchen was an annexe at the side of the bungalow, where their steward would do the cooking. Although they had running water for cooking and washing, their toilet was of the septic tank variety, since there was no mains sewerage on the campus. Although comfortable enough, life at Umuahia was quite a contrast to what they had left behind in England. The college supplied its own electricity from a generator, which was turned on when it got dark and off again at ten. Nobody ever turned their own lights off; they went to bed when the generator was shut down. A letter from Donald to his friend Philip Goodwin back at Clarendon Park, Leicester, written in November 1965, describes the way of life this forced upon them. The letter concluded: 'Well, our lights all go out at 10.00pm as we operate our own electric light generator on the Compound, and we can't afford to have it on longer than 6.30 to 10.00 in the evenings. So I will close before we are plunged into the semi-darkness of a kerosene lamp!'

Geoff Johnston, Donald's Presbyterian tutorial colleague at that time, now living in Ontario, Canada, remembers this clearly. He writes: 'The system worked well except on

Saints Days, when the Anglicans assembled in the Chapel for early morning communion. The organ ran on electricity, and the generator was turned on for the service. Of course, all the lights in the college came on and the somnolent Nonconformists were rudely awakened!' This gave rise on one occasion to some good-humoured banter between the college tutors. At a faculty meeting the week after St Patrick's Day, Donald asked on behalf of his Ulster-born wife, but with a twinkle in his eye: 'Why didn't the Anglicans have early morning communion to mark St Patrick's Day?' The Anglican Principal, Philip Ross, explained rather sheepishly: 'Patrick was only a black-letter saint and Anglican evangelicals restrict our observance of saints' days to red-letter saints only – those who are actually named in the Bible.' The meeting dissolved into laughter. The incident was typical of the open, easy-going and good-natured working relationship between the college tutors, to which Donald made such an important contribution.

Trinity Theological College was founded in 1948 to train clergy for the Anglican, Methodist and Presbyterian churches. It had started in temporary quarters at Awka and moved to the site on the outskirts of Umuahia two years later, in 1950. An archive note by Stanley Smith, held in the Methodist World Church Office, records that a site committee (of which Smith was a member) had explored a certain rainforest area on a sweltering hot day to find a suitable location for the venture, and that the first Principal (a Methodist minister, A.W. Hodgotts) not only taught theology but also had to supervise the construction of what became a fine suite of buildings in the clearing made in the forest. By the time Donald English arrived there in 1962 the college was well established.

Although Trinity was a 'Union' college, in its early days it had seemed more like three colleges, with three sets of students from three denominations being trained on the same compound. When Donald arrived, the senior Anglican, Canon Philip Ross, was Principal, and subsequently a second Presbyterian, Roy Gellatly, joined the staff to work alongside Geoff Johnston. By now the rather uneasy (though well-intentioned) inter-denominational relationships had disappeared, and Geoff Johnston describes a much happier regime:

> Philip ran the college as a kind of co-operative. He was very sensitive to the fact that it was a Union college, despite the preponderance of Anglicans among the student body. His collegial leadership was one with which Don and I were very happy. Indeed, it was a very happy staff, and much of the credit for that must also go to Don's easy, congenial style. He was a pleasure to work with, sympathetic and constructive.

Johnston recalls Donald at one staff meeting saying: 'The last thing we want here is some kind of "Anglimethoderianism"! We should all be ourselves and live with our differences as well as our commonalities.' Donald did insist that all Methodist students had to attend their Methodist class meeting, but in every other way he treated students as themselves, whatever their denomination. As Philip Ross put it in an article about the college for the January 1964 edition of *Kingdom Overseas*, the Methodist Missionary Society magazine:

> Perhaps one of the reasons why things work together so harmoniously in Trinity College is that we accept the fact that we come from different traditions, and we do not try to be anything but what we are. We have not sought to produce some synthesis which could only mean a watering down of each tradition, but have come to understand and appreciate the forms of worship of others.

Daily morning prayers in college rotated between the Anglican, Presbyterian and Methodist rites in turn, and as the students led in alphabetical name order regardless of their denomination they quickly became familiar with liturgies and practices other than their own. Evening prayers were led by the tutors, following the same system, and Geoff Johnston records wryly:

> Philip Ross made a good Presbyterian but a lousy Methodist! Looking back on it now I realise that he only seemed such a lousy Methodist because Donald was such a good one. Don's prayers were extempore, I guess in the Primitive tradition, but they were always relevant, literate and moving. He was a tough act to follow. The same could be said of his preaching. Good teachers are not always good preachers, but Don was. I looked forward to the days when he was to preach because I knew I would hear something I needed to hear.

Sunday Mbang, Prelate of the Methodist Church, Nigeria, and Chair of the World Methodist Council, was a student under Donald, and he writes:

> Dr Donald English came to Umuahai when Trinity College needed spiritual reformation; that is an atmosphere conducive to meaningful learning and positive strength for solid academic foundation for teaching and research. This outstanding religious leader at this early period of his ministerial journey was able to make his mark ... His worship services attracted crowds of people of all sexes, ages, class and nationality everywhere. Wherever and whenever Donald was scheduled or invited to preach, unless you were there thirty minutes before the start of the worship service you were unlikely to have a seat ... His home was open to us [students] anytime. He was in the habit of visiting us in our rooms regularly to pray with us, to

counsel us and to advise us in our spiritual and academic work. He encouraged all of us to aim higher in our academic pursuit and also to work very hard in our spiritual development.

Sunday Mbang also speaks of the way Donald assisted him in what would be his own significant academic journey.[2]

Someone else who spoke highly of Donald's preaching at that time was Kenneth Cracknell, a British Methodist minister who had gone out to Nigeria at the same time as Donald to serve as Chaplain and Lecturer at the Methodist College, Uzuakoli, some twenty miles from Umuahia. He recalls:

> Donald was a truly magnificent preacher in the context of Nigerian high school and college students in the sixties. At Uzuakoli we had some of most able students of their genera-tion, and many of them made profound Christian commit-ments while at school or college. Donald welcomed his participation in this evangelistic task and preached highly intelligent apologetics – with obvious great effect. I said to him on one occasion: 'Don't make an altar call, Donald, or we'll have the whole of the student body down the front, together with most of their teachers!' He never did (our students in Methodist College were already committed Christians), but one could see that our young men were profoundly influenced. I know he helped many in their discipleship, and not a few among those he helped are now bishops and leading laymen in the contemporary Nigerian Methodist Church.

Donald and Bertha had been in Nigeria for just over a year when their first son, Richard, was born, on 16 December 1963. A second son, Paul, was born two years later, on 27

---

[2] His Eminence Sunday Mbang to Brian Hoare, 14 November 2002.

August 1965. They took great delight in their two boys and the English family was extremely close from those earliest days onwards. The four of them enjoyed spending frequent weekends with the Cracknell family, either at Uzuakoli or Umuahia. Kenneth Cracknell had been the first among what he calls 'our crowd in Nigeria' to read the then-controversial book by Bishop John Robinson, *Honest to God*, and he lent Donald his copy, together with many other volumes of a more liberal persuasion.[3] 'We had a good deal of lively conversation about the prevailing theology of the sixties,' Kenneth writes:

> I conceived the highest opinion of his [Donald's] biblical scholarship and I suppose that Donald also learnt from me some things which he had missed out on in his early theological education: Wesley House was notorious at the time he was there for avoiding systematic and philosophical theology, and in those days conservative evangelicals also had a distinct aversion to speculative theology. But never did we have a cross word, and I have often reflected that our common Wesleyan Arminianism meant more to each of us than party labels like conservative evangelical or liberal/radical.

Donald had not been at Umuahia long before he was playing his part in the wider life of Nigerian Methodism beyond the college. At the 1962 Conference he was appointed to both the Candidates' Committee and the Doctrinal Appeals Committee.[4] He also found himself being drawn into the life of other denominations in Nigeria, and went to both the Anglican Diocesan Synod and the Presbyterian Synod to present

---

[3] J. Robinson, *Honest to God* (London: SCM, 1963). This book, setting out radical ideas about theology, was very widely read at the time.

[4] See *The Methodist Church, Nigeria: Minutes of Conference*, 1962 (Lagos, 1962).

the college's annual report to those bodies. Within the institutional life of the college, too, he took on increasing responsibility as time went on, and when Philip Ross went on leave Donald was appointed Acting Principal – a role he fulfilled competently and apparently without a hitch.

Bertha, meanwhile, was busy looking after the home and their two boys, Richard and Paul, but she still found time to lead a Sunday school on Sunday mornings for the children living in the college hostel. Jill Andrews, who had initially gone out to Nigeria to do teacher training at Oron, some eighty miles south of Umuahia, but was now teaching at the nearby Umuahia Primary School, recalls that Bertha asked her to help with that work in 1965. Jill became a great friend of the family, often staying with Bertha when Donald was away from the college. She wrote home in July 1965: 'I may be sleeping at Bertha's in August as Don will be away and she is expecting her second baby. She had to have Richard by Caesar op. and she wants someone there in case of complications.' Again, the following month, she wrote: 'I've been sleeping at Bertha's all this week, but fortunately the baby didn't show any signs of coming and now Don is home again. I was rather relieved not to have to act as midwife.' It was Jill who, many years later back in England, often looked after the Englishes' dog, Abigail, when they were away on Donald's preaching tours.

In addition to her Sunday school work, Bertha helped in the college office whenever she could. It was she who helped to train Felix Nwoke, a young clerk who had no secondary education, but who was eventually promoted to the post of bursar and later still entered the ordained ministry. As Betty Ross, Philip's widow, testifies: 'Donald and Bertha were both a tremendous asset at a time when the college was developing both numerically and academically.' She continues:

Donald was also a great support to my husband and to other members of staff, particularly at one period when we were dealing with some cases of immoral behaviour. On another occasion we heard from one of the students that an Anglican student who had been suspended was coming armed to the compound to shoot my husband. Donald persuaded Philip not to go to the office between lectures, but went himself instead. When the student arrived Donald persuaded him to give up the gun and they went into the chapel and prayed. Then he brought him to Philip and after more prayer the student went home.

Life at Umuahia was evidently never dull, and provided many memorable moments for Donald and Bertha. They recounted one such occasion in an article entitled 'Mercy Drops', which they wrote jointly for *Sound of Revival*, the magazine of the MRF, in 1964:

It happened on Easter morning. About 4.30am we were already awake when we heard the sound of distant singing somewhere on the other side of the compound. We rose quickly and went to the door, only to hear the singing coming nearer, and to see in the darkness before dawn a group of white-clad figures carrying bush lamps and approaching our house while they sang the joyful Ibo Easter hymns. A group of our students were keeping the lovely custom of greeting the Resurrection morning in this way. They sang at our house, their deep melodious voices thrilling with the joy and triumph of Easter Day.

We stood on our verandah and watched and listened while the dawn brought light. One could feel that the twenty centuries were as nothing in the face of the timeless truth of the Resurrection. Like the early disciples we knew the thrill of the Risen Christ. The cross could not finish him, the tomb could not hold him. Hallelujah, Christ is risen! We knew silent tears of joy at the wonder of it all, and we thanked God that the little boy [Richard] we were holding in our arms would grow up in a world which, despite all its wickedness, was the scene of this great and glorious Christ-event.[5]

Further insights into life at Umuahia are provided by a prayer tape that Donald recorded for prayer supporters in Britain. It focuses on the theme of Christian unity, something of great importance to Donald, and describes three different scenes:

The first scene can only be described as 'a harvest festival with a difference' at Trinity College. Staff and students gathered outside the college chapel on a warm sunny early evening in October. We were led by our Acting Principal, an experienced Anglican missionary. Thus began a service held almost entirely out of doors. After a prayer we marched in procession singing a hymn of praise to the part of the compound where the staff houses are. There we paused, heard a student read the story of creation from Genesis, particularly as it concerned the family, and a member of staff gave thanks for all the joys of love and family life. We ... moved on singing our next hymn. Our second stop was on the hillside overlooking the lovely expanse of wild bush stretching out for miles. Here the reading was a Psalm of praise for the created world, we had our prayers, sang a chorus and moved on again. Next we stopped at the students' dining hall, collected our fruit and vegetables, read and prayed appropriately and moved on with chorus and hymn. Finally we read and prayed outside the lecture rooms, and then entered the chapel, laid our gifts in front of the table and had our sermon and closing hymn.

The important thing about all this was the unselfconscious nature of our sharing together ... the Anglican led the procession, the Methodist preached and each denomination was represented in readings and prayers. The presence of a Ghanaian

---

[5] *Sound of Revival*, October 1964.

Presbyterian staff member added further variety. Through it all we felt our deep unity. The fact of our agreement on evangelical doctrine was a great help here.

The second scene requires a totally different background. Each year the staff and students of Trinity College go out on campaign in about six or eight teams. The teams work in certain churches by invitation, but the composition of the teams is inter-denominational. During the past year two teams worked in a Methodist circuit near Umuahia. Part of this circuit is in a remote area with very rough tracks as means of access. In the rainy season they become quite inaccessible. During the campaign there happened to be some heavy rain just before we were due to visit one small remote village. The local lay leader had pleaded for a visit and it mattered very much to him. So the minister, the catechist and I left the car as near to the village as we could, and trekked the rest of the way.

We duly reached the spot and after a word of prayer went into the little market where all the stall-holders were called to silence, and I began to speak through an interpreter of the purpose of the mission and the meaning of the gospel. I had hardly begun when out through a gap in the bush came our student leader, followed at intervals by each of the [rest of the] team. They had cycled so far, carried their bicycles another distance, then left them and walked the rest – in bare feet with shoes round their necks ... This is another aspect of our unity: the oneness of our determination to preach the riches of Christ to the uttermost parts of the world. Here it is not your denomination that matters, but your obedience to Christ's command.

The last scene is again of a different quality. You must now imagine a conference room with over thirty people seated around the table. Some are more easily recognisable than others. The Archbishop of the Province of West Africa, and a number of bishops, are present. The Moderator and Clerk of Synod of the Presbyterian Church, Nigeria lead the Presbyterian representation. The Methodist President and Chairman are present in addition to university lecturers in theology and theological college tutors. It is a unique occasion in Eastern Nigerian Church history. The purpose of the gathering is to consider major elements in theological college teaching. Many basic matters are discussed, and then well down the agenda comes the question of training the wives of students on the same compound. The missionary personnel speak enthusiastically for the project, if money can be found. Then a new note is sounded. One after another the Nigerian leaders rise to say that this is not the African way. The men should be separate for their training. What had appeared as a financial problem now becomes a matter of policy, and the Europeans are realising that this united church is, after all, Nigerian. It belongs to the Nigerians, not to us. Here is a third aspect of our unity, the unity of a church which becomes increasingly indigenous. The Nigerian Christians are, under God, responsible for it.

The political situation in Nigeria had been less than stable throughout Donald and Bertha's time there, but had not proved problematic as far as their life in Umuahia was concerned. Towards the end of their term of service, however, unrest was becoming evermore serious. Although this was not the reason for their return to circuit work in England (they had never intended to become long-term missionaries), they were nevertheless relieved in the end to be coming home, though sorry to be leaving behind the people who had made their time in Nigeria so special. Bertha had enjoyed Nigeria far less than Donald. She suffered badly from the insects and had malaria for a time. Nevertheless they had managed marvellously well to integrate into the Nigerian culture and lifestyle, and their boys, Richard and Paul, had never known anything else. Now it was a case of adjusting again to life in England. 'Our two boys are flourishing,' Donald wrote to Philip Goodwin. 'How they will take to the heavy clothing required for England remains to be seen! At present

Richard's only requirements are a pair of thin pants and a light shirt.'

Their last few weeks in Nigeria were not without incident. Jill Andrews wrote on 27 November 1965:

Don and Bertha had a false alarm this week. On Wednesday they heard from a visitor that the boat they had booked on, the *Ebani*, was leaving next Monday and they were expecting to leave on December 13. So they had to frantically get packed up whilst trying to find out if this was true. They couldn't find out until yesterday, and apparently ... they are really booked on the *Eboe* which does leave on December 13, so now they are all packed up and have another two weeks.

Only a week before they were due to sail, Jill Andrews recorded a further setback:

The Englishes had a nasty experience yesterday. They were having their farewell do at the college and I went up to baby sit for them, but they weren't in when I got there. They had gone to Enugu in the morning as Don was preaching at a wedding there, and on the way they had an accident with a cyclist. He turned right in front of them without any warning, fell on to the bonnet of the car, crashed into the windscreen, broke it and slid to the ground. He was only cut fortunately, and wasn't kept in hospital, but they were all shocked and had to give statements.

In the event it was decided that Donald had not been to blame and they were greatly relieved to be able to leave as planned – though their sailing was delayed until 16 December.

So the English family left Umuahia and set sail for a new stage in their lives, calling en route at Freetown, Sierra Leone, where another returning Methodist missionary, Roger Smith, embarked. He remembers the journey well:

Donald was returning from Nigeria with Bertha, and I joined the ship at Freetown. One of the perks of working in West Africa at that time was that you got a cruise into the bargain! Anyway, we played deck games, sunbathed and swam, relaxing after our strenuous work. Above all we talked, mostly telling each other stories about what we had done. My impression at the time was of an evangelical indeed, but so relaxed and at ease with God, himself and other people that it was just good to be with him. At a meeting when he was President he came over to me and started talking about the voyage as if it had been yesterday ...

Donald did not forget the situation he and his family had left behind in Nigeria. War finally broke out not many months after their departure, and lasted until 1970. Donald was at pains to keep in constant touch with the situation, particularly as the hostilities were coming uncomfortably close to the college where he had worked. Stanley Smith recorded what Donald passed on to him from his contacts back in Umuahia, and offered his own reflections upon it:

The people of the nearby village were concerned about some of the contents of the College Chapel, although many were not of the Christian faith. A village project was started to secure the safety of the communion rail and table, pulpit, lectern and font. They were all hand-carved from African oak (iroko wood). Invading armies loot and destroy, and they must light fires if they are to cook and eat. It was feared this finely carved work might become firewood. A deep and wide pit was dug – a lengthy task with only hand tools to use. The pit was lined with waterproof material of a native kind, and the sacred objects as well, before being placed within the pit. All was filled in – no mean feat, because Africans sense at once if ground has been disturbed. Therefore the camouflage must have been top quality. At the end of the hostilities, all was brought to the surface and found to be in perfect condition. In the tropical rain forest, where moisture is abundant and ants in quantity will search for and devour wood, this was an achievement. All was replaced in the renovated Chapel.[6]

* * * * *

Donald English's four years in Nigeria represented only a comparatively brief period in the context of his whole ministry, but it is worth asking what impact they had upon him and his subsequent work. Kenneth Cracknell (who is now a professor at Brite Divinity School, Texas Christian University, USA) provides the following reflection:

Donald's time in Nigeria was perhaps too short to have been a lasting influence upon his whole outlook on the Christian faith: it did not turn him, as it turned me ... to a supreme passion about the cross-cultural communication of the gospel ... But I think these years were formative in another direction, that of his outstanding leadership of world Methodism. Almost as soon as we arrived in Nigeria (August 1962) the old Eastern Nigeria District of the Methodist Church of Great Britain gave up its separate existence to join with the Western Nigeria District in the newly autonomous Methodist Church of Nigeria. Donald and I were present at the last meeting of the Eastern Nigerian District in Uzuakoli and the first meeting of the newly independent Nigerian Methodist Church in Lagos ... Considerable ecclesiastical statesmanship had been deployed by both westerners and easterners, both by Nigerians and by expatriates, and Donald was impressed (as we all were) by the quality of church leadership manifest at that time. I think he felt a real calling then to develop the same skills in

---

[6] Methodist World Church Office archives.

bringing a new sense of unity to the World Methodist Council
… as well as to British Methodism with all its diversities.

But that is to jump ahead. Donald's next step, in 1966, was
into circuit ministry.

4

Circuit Ministry

While Jean Alderson, a Methodist from Cullercoats, was in
Nigeria in 1965 visiting her daughter, Phoebe, who was
working in Ibadan, she happened to meet Donald and
Bertha English. They made an immediate impression on
her, not only because of the sort of people they were, but
also because, like her, Donald came from the north-east of
England. In the course of conversation she discovered that
they were soon due to leave Nigeria and were just beginning
the process of looking for a circuit appointment back in
England. On her return home to Cullercoats, a coastal town
near Newcastle upon Tyne, Jean told her husband, Fred, of
this encounter, and as he was one of the circuit stewards
responsible for finding a new minister he wrote to Donald
asking if he would consider an invitation to this appointment. It was a tempting prospect for Donald and his family
since Cullercoats was not far from Consett where he had
been brought up and where his parents still lived. So it
was that in August 1966 the English family arrived to make
their new home in the manse in Mast Lane. It was a happy
coincidence that one of Donald's first responsibilities was
to conduct the wedding of Phoebe Alderson and Dr Peter
Toft, whom she had first met in Nigeria.

Cullercoats Methodist Church was a large, imposing
modern building occupying a strategic corner site at a

crossroads on the Broadway. Stanley Lawson, the last surviving trustee of the board that originally planned the building of the church, recalled the many months of work involved with the then minister, Bill Dagg, and the architect on the design. The new church attracted good congregations and soon flourished under Bill Dagg's inspiring leadership. He was followed by another fine young minister, Geoffrey Buswell. When the time came for him to move on there was some understandable concern lest his successor should not be up to the task of continuing the splendid work done by these ministers in establishing a congregation which by now numbered 346 members. They need not have worried. As Stanley Lawson wrote: 'We were thrilled to know that a new young minister was coming to us from teaching in a theological college in Africa, and our hopes were more than fulfilled when Donald English started his ministry.' Not everyone in the circuit had been convinced at first, however. One of the other ministers commented: 'Oh, he's coming from the mission field, and you know what missionaries are like when they get back on the home front!' He quickly revised his opinion. The church was soon filled to capacity at every service Donald conducted, such was his wonderful preaching. Church membership continued to grow, reaching 425 within 4 years of Donald's arrival, and the Sunday school (in which he took a particular interest) became one of the largest in Methodism, with almost 400 children on its books.

December soon came, with all the usual Christmas festivities, and December 1966 was a special time for the English family, who had spent the previous four Christmases in Africa in a very different climate and culture. Ida Lawson recalls how just after midnight, as they finished the Christmas Eve service and were wishing each other a happy Christmas, someone shouted 'It's snowing!' and everyone gathered around the church porch. Donald was thrilled to see the snow, and said 'Come on, let's sing *O Come, All Ye Faithful*', which they did with great joy and feeling. Says Mrs Lawson: 'It was something special: the large street lamps cast a golden glow on the snow and the fairy lights and Christmas trees twinkled in the windows of the houses around. It was the beginning of many happy times we shared.'

The following year, such were the numbers wanting to come to church on Christmas Eve that Donald instituted a continuous communion with no formal service led from the front, but only pew leaflets to help those attending to think about the meaning of Christmas and an invitation to come forward to receive bread and wine whenever they were ready to do so. The carol service, too, became an increasingly popular service, so much so that two services had to be held, at 5.00pm and 7.00pm, with the sound relayed into the church hall – and even then people were standing in the vestibule. Another tradition begun in Donald's time as minister was an 8.00am half-hour communion service each Sunday, which included a short five-minute sermon – perhaps a precursor of his expertly crafted three-minute 'Thought for the Day' talks appreciated by so many BBC Radio Four listeners many years later. There was one never-to-be-forgotten occasion on which the service was due to start but there was no sign of Donald. One of the stewards went to the manse just down the road only to find he had overslept and was still in bed.

As he became established at Cullercoats Donald began increasingly to shape both his own ministry and the life of the church in new ways. He had a clear vision and was constantly leading, even pushing, the church towards its fulfilment. He started a church fellowship in an attempt to unite people from all the various groups, activities and departments of the church. There were the resource groups he began in order to bring together people from different

areas of working life for mutual support and encouragement. They included groups for church members working
in the worlds of business, communications, education,
health and welfare, cutting right across the normal church
groupings, which tended to be by age or gender. In addition
to their value to church members themselves, these resource
groups also had an outreach element, for they were the sort
of meetings to which non-church work colleagues could be
invited without fear of embarrassment. Indeed, outreach
beyond the church was a major motivation in Donald's
ministry. One member recalls him once saying: 'You can't
get people to come in and do things if they are sitting around
on hard chairs. If you held this meeting in the pub up the
road where it is warm and comfortable then they might be
more likely to come.' Today the church has a pleasant
carpeted lounge with comfortable easy chairs, which was
opened for its silver jubilee as a direct result of the vision
formulated during Donald's ministry.

The Cullercoats church had a comparatively new council
housing estate almost on its doorstep, and Donald never
allowed his congregation to overlook the fact that this presented both a pastoral and a missionary challenge to the
church. The young adults on one occasion noted where the
church members actually lived on a street plan of the area
and discovered what they described as 'a great mass of
nothing' on that estate. Despite the fact that the church was
drawing large congregations, very few people came from
the council housing. In an attempt to reach out to the community around the church, Donald organised house-to-
house visitation of the area jointly with St George's, the parish church on the seafront. Visitors went out in pairs and,
although many felt nervous at the prospect, the preparation
Donald gave them and the inspiration he provided soon put
them at their ease. One church member recalls how she
and a friend were explaining their reticence to him and

confessing how tongue-tied they became when visiting strangers. Donald responded: 'Well, you can't expect it to be an easy task, but you must tell the Lord about it. You don't need to speak out loud, but just tell him that you can't cope and ask him to be with you, to put the right words into your mouth and to help you. Talk to the Lord as if you were talking to a friend right next to you.'

In a further attempt to reach out to the community, both to the inhabitants of Cullercoats itself and to holiday-makers who came to what was quite an attractive seaside town, Donald started a series of open-air meetings during the summer months. These would include music, drama and testimony, and he would always speak, again demonstrating his considerable gifts as an evangelist. There is little evidence that these meetings led to new people coming to the church, but they undoubtedly put the local Methodists on the map and gave many members of the congregation a greater sense of confidence in the task of evangelism.

Along the seafront from the site of these open-air meetings was a Methodist guest house (now sold and used as a residential home), and Donald made a habit of visiting it every Saturday evening to welcome the new guests and invite them to worship at the Methodist church. This swelled the congregations during the holiday season and perhaps also sowed the seeds of his preaching becoming more widely known around the Methodist Connexion. Holidaymakers would return home and enthuse about the preacher they had heard in Cullercoats, and invitations to Donald to preach in other parts of the country began to increase.

It was Donald who was largely responsible for developing good relationships between the Methodists and St George's. In the last two years that Donald was at Cullercoats, the Vicar of St George's was David Lunn (who was later to become the Bishop of Sheffield), and he and Donald worked particularly happily together. Anglican–Methodist relationships had not been nearly as close when Donald first arrived. The Anglican incumbent at that time was Father George Chadwick, a High Churchman. However, in June 1969, the two churches did hold a joint garden party on Links Avenue playing field, just off Broadway. In a joint message in the programme for that event Donald and George Chadwick wrote:

We are more than pleased that the warmth of friendship between our two congregations has led to the planning of this joint Garden Party. It could be said to have two purposes: firstly, that we find the joy and pleasure in God's wonderful world that we are meant to find; and secondly, that we find it together and in so doing get to know one another even better than we do already.

The 1969 garden party, although the first joint Anglican–Methodist event, was not the first garden party to be held. That had been a much smaller Methodist venture in 1966, the summer before Donald's arrival, and it had made a loss. The following year, 1967, Donald concentrated more on giving it the feel of a big church family get-together, a social event for members and their families and friends, and he had more ambitious plans. The Links playing field seemed an ideal location, and Donald approached the local council for permission to use it. As a church member at the time put it: 'That was a time when you needed Donald behind you to do something. The council said we could have it free of charge so long as we didn't charge for admission – so Donald said we'd sell programmes instead!' The event was a great success, with three large marquees, a brass band and a cricket match (in which Donald played a major role). Hundreds of people attended. It was following this successful venture that St George's was invited to share in the next garden party two years later. Joint garden parties are one thing, however; joint worship is quite another. It was not until Father Chadwick was succeeded by David Lunn that things began to move forward on that level. Donald and David not only exchanged pulpits, but the Methodist congregation was welcomed to share in Holy Communion at St George's. Donald would appear in his black preaching gown, which contrasted starkly with the vicar's white robes. Many members of the congregation remember how he would stride up the aisle so quickly that his gown billowed out behind him. As he joked afterwards, 'I was playing the Devil's advocate!'

Never content simply to keep things ticking over, Donald continued to initiate other new ventures at Cullercoats. Writing to the church members in 1969 he said: 'There are so many things which God has given us to do for Him in this area and the time has come to re-assess how much more we could make possible by reviewing our offers of time, talents and money.'[1] One new venture was a Sunday night fellowship for young people, which normally met at the manse, but on other occasions in different members' homes. There was a growing number of young people attached to the church at that time and meetings were well supported, particularly during vacations, when those who were away at college returned home. They were able to discuss and debate any topic. Donald's guidance and support helped many young people with their future lives.[2] Two members of the fellowship at that time, Trevor and Margaret Kingsley-Smith, who were married by Donald in 1972, speak warmly of his pastoral help and support during their years of separation as students at Newcastle University and

[1] Donald English to Cullercoats Methodist Church members, 28 August 1969.

[2] L. Osborn, 'Donald English – Pastor' in Abbott (ed.), *Donald English*, p. 17.

University College Hospital, London, respectively. They
also recall with gratitude the welcome they always received
at the manse from Bertha English, whose single word of
greeting – 'Welcome!' – was always said with a warmth and
sincerity that made a deep impression on them. Indeed,
Bertha constantly supported and complemented Donald's
ministry in Cullercoats. As well as her involvement with
the youth fellowship, she always stood at the church door
beside Donald to greet people at the end of services, but was
also a gifted local preacher in her own right, and often
spoke at the Women's Fellowship and Young Wives'
Group. She was a tower of strength to Donald, and he often
acknowledged his gratitude for her support and love publicly from the pulpit.

Another of Donald's initiatives was a playgroup for
pre-school children, one of the first church-based play-
groups in the area. This, in turn, fed the growth of the
Sunday school, to which reference has already been made.
Indeed, its very success led to problems, for a waiting list
had to be started for the beginners' department, and some
children got quite upset that there was not yet room for
them. In an attempt to address the problem, Donald
approached Evelyn Horsey, a retired teacher living on her
own, and persuaded her to start up a pre-Sunday school
group to cater for these children. She enjoyed it greatly and
continued the group until there was no longer a waiting
list. Her devoted work brought her into contact with many
families. When she died following a spell in hospital,
Donald recounted in his sermon how, although she had no
relatives of her own, she received more visitors than anyone else in the ward because of the great affection in which
she was held by the playgroup parents.

During these years the Sunday school grew to over 400
children with a staff of between 60 and 70 teachers, and this
led to some practical difficulties over accommodating so

many people on the church premises.[3] Eventually the trust-
ees applied to the local council for permission to erect a
large wooden classroom in the church grounds as a temporary measure for one year – and it is still there over thirty
years later! The large numbers made events like Promotion
Sunday (when children progressed from one department of
the Sunday school to the next) particularly difficult. With
the normal congregation swollen by proud parents, the
children queued down the aisles of the church and along the
pathways outside to hear their names called and be received
by their new teachers. Although usually all went smoothly,
that Sunday earned the nickname 'Commotion Sunday'.

With such a large Sunday school staff, Donald always
stressed the importance of their regular meetings for preparation, meetings he himself would often attend. He had a
wonderful ability to take the lesson themes for all the various departments and expound them simply and clearly in
ten minutes. When he spoke to the children themselves, that
ability was evident at a very different level. One teacher
recalls the impact made by a talk he gave based on the Rolf
Harris song 'Two Little Boys', which was popular at the
time, and what he made of the line about there being room
on the horse for two.

Donald had a genuine love for children and enjoyed
spending time with them whenever he could. A memory recorded by Betty Smith illustrates the fact well. The Smith
family and the English family for two years running had co-
incidentally arranged summer holidays to Coleraine, Northern Ireland, where Betty's husband, Westley, had been born
and brought up and where Bertha had been evacuated to live
with relatives during the Second World War. They naturally
arranged to meet, and Betty recounts what happened:

[3] A peak was reached in 1970 to 1971 with 409 scholars on the
books. Average attendance was 277.9: 'Cullercoats Methodist
Church Sunday School, Statistical Report, 1972/73'.

We have vivid memories of Don and Bertha with Richard and Paul, together with my husband and I and our five-year-old daughter Maureen walking through Down-Hill Forest on a glorious summer afternoon. As we walked along the edge of a sparkling lake in this idyllic setting a rather large log appeared in the distance. The children lost no time in resting on it, and started singing the 'Frog' nursery song. Don immediately joined them and they chorused together:

Four little speckled frogs sat on a speckled log
munching some most delicious bugs, yum! yum!
One jumped into the pool, where it was nice and cool;
then there were only three-ee speckled frogs.
Three little speckled frogs ...

Betty Smith continues:

Each one in turn jumped off the log amid shrieks of laughter. It was a sight to behold! As we stood bemused at the sight of three small children and one grown man mimicking the antics of frogs, Bertha said: 'This will go into a sermon, you know.' I never heard if it did.

At the other end of the age range, Donald had an equally genuine concern for older people. In one church meeting, as the needs of the elderly in the area were discussed, he made the observation: 'Behind all those pristine net curtains there's a lot of loneliness.' He was subsequently approached by the local social services to see whether the church might be willing to start a luncheon club for the elderly. This approach came at the same time as Donald was wondering how he might use the gifts of a lady in the church who had just retired and was looking for some form of service to occupy her time and energy. He was adept at delegation, and soon Dora Wilson, the lady in question, was in charge of a flourishing luncheon club, which became her whole life – visiting potential members, preparing for the weekly meetings and giving herself fully to developing this new activity.

All this activity in a large church inevitably demanded a great deal of administrative skill, and in order to cope with it Donald instituted a regular monthly stewards' meeting. Since everyone's time was precious, not least his own, it was difficult to come up with a good time for this meeting. As everyone had to eat, Donald suggested that stewards and their spouses should meet for tea at 5.00pm and finish at 7.30pm, when he would invariably dash off to whatever other meeting required his presence that evening. One of the stewards at that time recalls, however, that 'When the meeting was at our house we never got started on time because Donald had to go out in the garden and play football with my five-year-old!' Due to the severe back pain from which Donald suffered occasionally, on one occasion when he was flat on his back the stewards' meeting took place around his bed.

The stewards' meeting evolved into a church leadership team, and would discuss the whole range of church activities, vacancies for a variety of church appointments and plans for special events. If a special Sunday service was planned, Donald would gather everyone involved to go through every detail, so that it would all run smoothly. He was a stickler for good preparation. Everybody knew exactly what he or she had to do, and nothing was left to chance. The stewards also served as a support and advice group for Donald, a function that became all the more important as demands on his time and energies grew not only within the local circuit but in wider Methodism. He was receiving a growing number of invitations as a speaker and as his gifts became increasingly recognised he was facing more and more demands on his time at District and national level. Although he turned down quite a number of requests himself, it was also useful to be able to discuss others with his stewards. One such invitation was to return as a visitor to the Methodist Conference in Nigeria (an obviously tempting prospect), but as this clashed with what would be the first church anniversary during his ministry in Cullercoats, the stewards advised him against going. He turned the invitation down. Nevertheless, the tensions of coping with the demands of an active, growing church and playing his part in the life of the denomination nationally would not go away. Indeed, they were destined to grow as the years went by and his ministry became even more widely recognised.

It was not only invitations to speak or to serve on a variety of committees that came Donald's way. Many people wrote to him for advice on personal matters. The following detailed response to the points raised in one such letter from a friend seeking his counsel, as a fellow evangelical, on the possibility of offering as a candidate for the ministry reveals something of Donald's own view of the task of a Methodist minister. If the language is less inclusive than would have been the case in his later years (for he was always very careful on that score) it is simply because he was writing before the possibility of women becoming Methodist ministers had become a reality:

Very many thanks for your letter which arrived today. It is kind of you to write that I need not reply at once; but my experience is that if I leave it there is no telling when there will be time again – so here goes!

Your paragraph about wanting to do the work, and feeling that you should do more than simply teaching, might have been an account of my own position ten years ago! And these are vital considerations. After all, you will have to *like* whatever work you do, and I gave up long ago believing that the Lord was determined to make us do what we don't wish to do, and to prevent us from doing what we do wish to do! He often has to do so, but it is preferable from everyone's viewpoint when His people want to do what is the right thing for them. And if He has been Lord of your life in the past it follows that He has been preparing you for the next step; a preparation which includes your feeling about what you want to do, and what you feel would be too much of a limitation, too. So to have a desire for the work is a very important clue. Your desire will, in any case, be tested and balanced by the judgement of the Church on your feeling.

As far as exercising a 'spiritual' ministry is concerned I don't see how any man can be prevented from exercising one in our ministry. This depends upon the man himself. One may not be able to exercise a ministry exactly in the way which one would like, but then I doubt whether anyone can. For example, a Methodist Minister is expected to chair a large number of business meetings, though I myself feel that these, too, are training grounds for our people (and for the minister!) in Christian grace and wisdom. The large number of churches also spreads a man's influence where he might prefer a concentration. In both these cases, however, Methodism is well aware of the problem, and there is legislation coming before the next Conference to simplify local church government by providing only five main committees, of which the Minister need chair only two. Let me make clear that there is still some frustration involved here, but one has to accept that no situation is without frustration, and this is part of ours. To know that the Lord understands and will help us with priorities is a great comfort.

Another source of frustration is named as the lack of lay leadership which one can really rely upon. The origins of this justifiable complaint are a bit obscure. One element is certainly that our lay folk simply are not instructed in the faith, and cannot be expected to be reliable leaders, therefore. But this is our opportunity. I fear that some ministers want a keen lay leadership, but only one which will be subservient to the minister! This isn't my reading of the ministry. If you want reliable lay leadership you have to give it its head. IVF and student leadership is a perfect illustration here, over against SCM with its resident Staff.

The itinerant system *has* its weaknesses, but I think it is fair to say that the tendency now is towards a longer stay than used to be the practice. And for us it simply means that we have to gear up our ministry to a five year stay in any one place, and to plan accordingly. I'm not sure that the old Class Meeting will ever be revitalised in modern Methodism. The climate of opinion, and the structure of society in many places, renders it very difficult to introduce with success. But some form of small group activity is necessary, and each area must work out what best suits its needs. A mid-week study group *is*, however, as you say, a vital addition to an itinerant ministry.

I suspect that the greatest source of frustration of all is the fact that the minister's life is crowded by 'potential' opportunities, and that there are three things requiring to be done at any given time. A multiplicity of small jobs can be a frustrating thing, and I suspect that this is what men mean when they say that they leave the ministry to do a 'man-sized job'. I cannot but feel that they reveal their inability to do one, because the ministry requires of a man a far greater sense of priorities, and determination to observe them within a fluid framework of life, than any other calling. You can manipulate books, timetables, machines, etc., but you never know what people will do! And people, bless them, are our job!

One last thing concerns the place of conservative evangelicals in Methodism. We must begin with the assumption that our position will not be known to many of our people, and that it will be suspected by some for that reason. We must also realise that people cannot be expected to grasp immediately what we are after, nor to accept our way of doing things at once. Even basic things like prayer and Bible study are extremely strange to many a modern Methodist, and it takes time to change this. At the same time our people, by dint of much variety, *do* recognise a conscientious minister when they see one, and they do appreciate a preacher who is trying to say something very basic which relates to everyday life at a spiritual level, and who gives himself to them 'unconditionally' (whether they dot his conservative 'i's and cross his evangelical 't's or not). This is the risk we have to take: to give ourselves to people in faith that the Lord can use us, *inside* Methodism, to change people and churches by the exposition and application of scriptural teaching to everyday life.

I take this to mean that we have to proceed with great care and understanding, like any teacher with a new class, not expecting more than can legitimately be expected, and not getting too worked up about things which we do not like. Before we come to the particular church they have been in it for years, and when we have gone they will be left to carry it on. You cannot blame them if they suspect wholesale changes at the outset of a man's ministry. They have seen it so many times before! So we need to be known first, as loving, spiritual and self-giving pastors whose task is to bring men and women to Christ, to build up the believers in a faith which is relevant, and to preach God's Word faithfully and clearly.

And it means that we have to choose our battles very carefully, and to see the task as one of education rather than coercion. Our aim is to teach and convince so that people want what is right, rather than having it thrust upon them as right, and then discovering it to be so. It also means that we have to be prepared to limit ourselves very largely to work within Methodism, and not to be dashing off to all kinds of non-Methodist activity where things are more congenial. It means that we must be willing to accept responsibility at Circuit, District, and, if invited, Connexional level, and to play our part in the debates at each level, not fearing to be involved. It may often bring us into compromised situations – committee work inevitably does, but I feel we must be ready for it if our voices are to be heard. Perhaps we have not been so well received in the past *because* our voices have not been heard, e.g. at Conference, until very recently.

Well, you may feel that this is more suited to a meeting of Methodist Ministers already in the fray, but I feel you should know all this, too. This is what you are being led into, and you may as well know it now. I close this description by saying that at this moment I would not wish to be in any other calling, or any other denomination, or any other church, than the one I am in. There *are* frustrations, but I believe that we are already seeing signs that the simple explanation of the gospel, and exercising of a caring ministry, is used by the Lord wherever we are. It is, after all, His work.[4]

As that letter reveals, Donald knew that one of the secrets of building up a strong church was the quality of the pastoral oversight he offered as a 'loving, spiritual and self-giving pastor', and he made every effort to make this a priority. He had a great gift for making people feel they mattered, and testimonies abound to his very personal approach and his ability to remember names and details: 'He christened both my children, and you felt it was the only christening he had ever done' … 'We'd only just moved in and as the removal van drove away Donald English called on us.' Another woman remembers Donald visiting her in hospital after her first child had been born. There was a sixteen-year-old Catholic girl in the next bed and Donald chatted to her as well – something that made a huge impression on her, especially as her own priest had not been to visit her. Donald was very good at keeping a note of people who were ill, and passed their names on to the lady in charge of the church flower rota, not only on Sundays, but throughout the week. If the church flowers had all been distributed he insisted

---

[4] Letter to Brian Hoare, 2 February 1967.

that more be bought so that no one missed out – and if the sick person was a man, he would often receive a basket of fruit instead. 'It's important that we show people we care,' Donald would say. There were inevitably some who grumbled from time to time that he hadn't visited them, but they were the people who expected a pastoral visit for no other reason than the fact that they were on the membership list. Donald's priorities, however, were first and foremost the bereaved, the sick and those with particular needs and problems. If time was left for more general visiting after that, then it was done; but in a church the size of Cullercoats that was only rarely possible.

Another member of the congregation at that time tells how her eldest son, Philip, became a member of the Cullercoats church during Donald's ministry, but subsequently drifted away. When, some twenty years later, Donald returned as a visiting preacher, however, Philip attended the service. Shaking Donald's hand at the door after the service, he said, 'I'm Philip Smith,' and went to move on out of the church. Donald pursued him, leaving the many others waiting to greet him, and said quietly, 'Philip, I still pray for you.' Philip had been going through a difficult time and was very impressed at such personal concern. This experience was a major factor in his return to the church. It is clear that such prayerfulness was another major factor in the effectiveness of Donald's ministry. Bertha once confided to a friend what he himself would never have divulged: that he had every member of the church listed on different days in his diary, and prayed daily for them.

When, after six full and happy years, the time came for Donald and Bertha to leave Cullercoats for other work, the church presented them with a freezer (quite a luxury in those days) and a generous cheque, and Donald was absolutely overwhelmed at the presentation. Such was his self-effacing humility that he apparently had no idea how

warmly people felt about him and his ministry. Yet, for all
the effective good work that his predecessors Bill Dagg and
Geoffrey Buswell had done, it was really Donald who laid
the foundations of the church as it developed and is today.

If George Bernard Shaw's adage 'He who can, does. He
who cannot, teaches' was ever true of anyone, it certainly
did not apply to Donald English. His move from circuit
work into what can be seen as the more rarefied world of
theological college teaching was simply in response to the
call of the church, and in no way because of any unsuitability
for front-line circuit ministry. He had already proved himself
a gifted and popular circuit minister, and now those gifts
were to be applied in a very different setting.

5

Theological Teacher

There were two periods in his life when Donald English was a theological teacher in England, from 1960 to 1962 and from 1972 to 1982. After having been accepted as a candidate for the Methodist ministry, Donald, as we have seen, did his theological training at Wesley House, Cambridge, and in 1960 he was appointed Assistant Tutor at Wesley College, Headingley, Leeds. It was very unusual in that period for someone so strongly influenced by the IVF and committed to the conservative evangelical tradition to be appointed to such a position. Indeed there was some hostility to conservative evangelicals training in the colleges. But those who feared that Donald's appointment would expose the Methodist ministerial students to a narrow-minded and fundamentalist form of evangelicalism were quickly proved wrong. The Methodist scholar Professor Peter Stephens, who knew Donald in those days, records the observation that Donald had as many, if not more, books from the SCM Press on his shelves as those from the Inter-Varsity Press and other evangelical publishers, and this typified his desire to engage with a whole range of theological views other than his own. He was anxious that the faith he held would not be isolated from the insights of other traditions, and he never then nor ever subsequently shirked encounter with those who were critical of his own understanding of the nature of Scripture. In this chapter

we will look at some of the concerns he addressed during his
years as a college tutor.

*   *   *   *   *

As well as being committed to theological exploration,
Donald was deeply concerned for the spiritual life of the
students. He did not see theology and spirituality as being in
conflict. In 1960, in an article for Christian Unions within
teacher training colleges, he wrote: 'May it not be that much
of our public failure is due to our unwillingness to face the
real issues and win the victory at the level of the will in our
prayer life?'[1] Donald was especially concerned, as a tutor in
a Methodist theological college, that fewer people were
coming forward for training for Methodist ministry, and he
saw this as being in part due to a general unwillingness to be
committed to God's guidance. In 1961, writing for Wesley
College, Headingley, about the downward trend in students
training for Methodist ministry (down from 150 in 1958 to
101 in 1961), he said: 'The main thing is to be ready to be
called, to face up to the great need of the Church, to seek
God's guidance in this matter and to be ready to commit oneself to action if his leading seems to be in this direction.'
There was no doubt in Donald's mind that this could be
costly. But he was determined to put across the message that
'as those for whom Christ died we have no room for hanging
back because a particular piece of service is costly. In front of
the Cross of Christ who will be the first to speak of cost?'[2]

There is also evidence in what he wrote at this stage that
Donald English was thinking seriously about issues connected with the wider Methodist denomination. This wider
vision would become increasingly important in his ministry.

---

[1] D. English, 'The Days of His Flesh', *TCCU Supplement*,
Autumn 1960, p. 7.
[2] Notes by D. English entitled 'Feed my Sheep' (December 1961).

'What is the true position', he asked, 'of the Minister in Methodist thinking?' As he considered the situation in the early 1960s he saw the need for a reappraisal. For some people the minister was a 'super-Christian'. This Donald denied. He also opposed the idea that the minister was 'a disguised layman'. While affirming the doctrine of the priesthood of all believers, he wished to make a distinction between the ordained minister and the lay person. To fulfil the ministry of the church, he argued, 'the Church is used of God to appoint men, in His Name, to the task of leading the Church, building up the faithful and seeking to bring in those outside'. Donald's references to 'men' in the ministry reflect the era in which he was writing. Later he was to affirm women in ordained Methodist ministry.[3] His call in the 1960s for people of ability and devotion to embody an attractive form of ministry, however, could apply to men or women. The possibility that excited Donald as a young tutor was that gifted young Christians who might have a good career before them in a professional job would none the less consider the ordained ministry. He lamented the fact that there was an impression that ministry was for 'second-rate' types and he looked for the best people to offer themselves. 'Unless Methodism receives a larger number of men of this calibre for her ministry', he commented, 'her work is certain to suffer.'[4]

In this period, as throughout his life, Donald English worked hard to understand and appreciate theological positions other than his own, but without ever losing his own theological integrity. His personal views were outlined in an article he wrote in 1961 for Christian Unions within technical colleges. His subject was the meaning of the atonement. It was not enough, he argued, to preach the fact of the

---

[3] Women were not admitted to the ordained ministry of the Methodist Church until 1973.

[4] Notes by D. English entitled 'Feed my Sheep' (December 1961).

cross. 'That stark fact', he insisted, '*must* be interpreted and given meaning.' Donald spoke about 'the various interpretations of that event given us in Scripture' and warned that the 'welter of contending theories of atonement must not be allowed to excuse our trying to understand what the cross means'. The first assertion Donald made was that the cross was exemplary. He spoke of the need to 'forward Christ's redemptive work in the world'. No Methodist, whatever their theology, would have disagreed with that view. Donald's second point was that the death of Christ was victorious. Again he applied this to the life of the Christian, and again this was a view that would have been widely acceptable. The final point, that Christ's death was sacrificial, led Donald to assert 'with as much delicacy and careful definition as possible, that the thing which He did for us, and which we could not do for ourselves, was the bearing upon Himself of the consequences of our sin, these consequences stemming from our having placed ourselves under the divine wrath against sin'.[5] This was a nuanced expression of the conservative evangelical belief in substitutionary atonement.

It was inevitable that Donald English would have to reflect on the set of beliefs that characterised conservative evangelicalism now that he found himself teaching in an environment in which the avowal of such beliefs was not common. As we have seen, he was always open to discussing with those of other views, and wished to present a credible account of his faith to those who did not see things as he did. The writers whom he recommended on the atonement included the Methodist Vincent Taylor, the Presbyterian James Denney and the Anglican Leon Morris. These represented a breadth of evangelical thinking. On the question of the interpretation of the early chapters of Genesis, Donald was similarly wider in his thinking than some evangelicals. He insisted that

---

[5] D. English, 'Obedient unto Death', *TCCU Supplement*, Spring 1961, pp. 5–9.

Genesis was 'pre-scientific and popular', came from the cultural forms of its author and did not propose a view on which the scientist could pronounce since it was making statements about, for example, humanity made in the image of God. 'The scientist, as such', he stated in 1962, 'cannot prove or disprove the Genesis assertions about God as Creator.' Donald made no attempt to defend the idea of a literal understanding of Genesis, but said that it was the job of the theologian to understand the literary form of the creation passages and the purpose for which they were written.[6]

After the two years of teaching at Headingley, Donald and Bertha, as outlined in Chapter 3, went to Nigeria for four years, where Donald was also a theological teacher. We have examined the six years, from 1966 to 1972, spent at Cullercoats. From 1972 Donald embarked on what would be ten years of sustained work as a Methodist theological tutor. He was appointed to the Lord Rank Chair of Historical Theology at Hartley Victoria College, Manchester. Peter Stephens remembers the Hartley Victoria Principal, Percy Scott, saying that he wanted Richard Jones on the staff as a radical, Stephens himself as someone in the central Methodist tradition and Donald as an evangelical. Donald was the only one of these three men that Scott had not had previously as a student or as a colleague and thus Donald's appointment is evidence of the impact made on Percy Scott by Donald. The decision by Percy Scott was to prove decisive for Donald's later ministry. Scott was an exception as a Methodist college principal in this period in seeking to have a staff that included the conservative evangelical element. A student of that time, Bob Kitching, recalls that evangelical students at Hartley Victoria were told by Scott that they were not to gather around Donald like 'wasps around a jam pot'. When he

---

[6] *Advance*, 8 February 1962, p. 2.

heard about this comment, Donald was at first rather hurt, but then later amused by the idea. It did illustrate the sensitivity there was at that time about the presence on the college staff of an avowedly conservative evangelical.

Although Donald spent only one year at Manchester, it was a significant year. One student, Trevor Noble, describes it in this way:

> I was 51 years old and a student in Hartley Victoria College in 1971–2 when following the Christmas break Donald English arrived as a tutor amid great excitement. I had a number of one to one sessions with him. At the time I had a full set of Wesley's Journals which I offered him in exchange for any of his books. Part of the bargain also was that when I was in Circuit he would come and preach in one of my churches.

Later, when Donald was Methodist President, he was able to do this. Bob Kitching says that Donald left his mark on the student body. He describes how he and Bertha and their two young sons entered fully into college life and also into the local Moss Side–Whalley Range community. As a way of building up the fellowship in the college, they had groups of students to their home for tea. Graham Slater, Methodist chaplain to students in Manchester, enlisted Donald to speak at a Lent school for students. Donald, as usual, had links beyond Methodism, preaching at St Edmund's Church of England in Whalley Range, speaking at Theological Students' Fellowship meetings (the TSF was an arm of the IVF), and helping to arrange a conference for Manchester TSF students. His commitment to the inter-denominational evangelical world continued.

Some notes that Donald wrote in that period illustrate his thinking about the relationship between Methodism and the broader evangelical tradition as it related to ministerial training. He was concerned to clarify what was meant by evangelical theology, to test its relevance in the modern world, and to look at all of this in the context of Methodist history, doctrine and practice. He was interested in the rise of Methodism, its historical, cultural and religious setting, and the nature of Methodist evangelical convictions in relation to evangelical and non-evangelical beliefs outside Methodism. Working from the historical study of Methodist developments, Donald was deeply committed to contemporary analysis, looking at evangelical doctrines and practices in the light of the current religious and cultural setting in the 1970s. He was especially concerned about the impact of the ecumenical movement and the charismatic movement, the place of dialogue with other religions, the influence of the behavioural sciences and questions posed by humanism and communism. It was against this background that Donald wished to examine the validity of evangelical experience and doctrine. To make the evangelical stance central, he argued, could be justified on historical and theological grounds as reflecting 'the heart of our Methodist heritage'.[7]

One way in which Donald attempted to put this philosophy about Methodism into practice at Hartley Victoria was by putting on a course covering the 'Constitutional Practice and Discipline of the Methodist Church'. Peter Stephens remembers Percy Scott's amazement that students wanted to attend what was a voluntary course on such a subject.[8] Scott was committed to the Methodist tradition, but was more concerned with the spirit of this than with the letter. Donald believed that students needed to be fully rooted in the concrete outworking of the Methodist tradition in order to be effective as ministers within the denomination, and so the emphasis of his course was on understanding the nature of Methodist ministry practically.

---

[7] Personal papers, 1974.

[8] Interview with Professor Stephens conducted by Graham Turner, 2001.

He was convinced that a study of constitutional practice and discipline – including an examination he set on it – helped in this process, and evidently his students also became convinced. No doubt they were influenced by his own enthusiasm.

At this point, many within Methodism assumed that Wesley College, Bristol, would be closed, and that the Bristol students would be transferred to Hartley Victoria. A commission that had been looking at the Methodist colleges in the light of falling numbers of ministerial students had recommended this option. At Conference, which had the final decision, it was expected that the decision by the commission would be rubber-stamped. In fact a major debate took place on the colleges and the voting was 303 in favour of Manchester and 303 in favour of Bristol. Harry Morton, as President of Conference (later General Secretary of the British Council of Churches) was asked by some to give the casting vote. Kenneth Greet, as Secretary of Conference, instead suggested that after tea there should be another vote by ballot (the first had been by a show of hands). This was done and by eleven votes Bristol carried the day in the ballot. Following the decision Harry Morton wrote to John A. Newton, who was teaching in Kenya, to ask if he would come back in 1973 to be Principal at Bristol. Newton's view was that younger tutors who had been appointed to Manchester should be transferred to Bristol. That thinking was followed and so Donald was transferred to Wesley College, Bristol, to the Lord Rank Chair of Practical Theology and Methodism.

In his one year at Hartley Victoria it was not possible for Donald English to translate his thinking into action to the extent that he would have wished. However, the move to Wesley College, Bristol, gave him scope to put his own distinctive stamp on areas of ministerial training. He was happy to work as part of a stimulating team. Newton saw his colleagues as such a talented group that any one of them could have been Principal. He described Donald as extremely loyal and supportive. Donald had his own convinced position, but in the context of a team of seven tutors, among whom there was considerable variation in terms of churchmanship, Donald was viewed as an irenical person. There were some strong personalities in the group and Donald was a reconciling force. He was always, Newton recalls, seeking to find a way in which the team members could come together and make a decision, which could then be implemented. It is significant that an evangelical should play this role within a group that included both conservative and radical figures. It seems that Donald's Methodist evangelicalism, as well as his own personality, contributed to this broad vision.

One study course at Bristol that allowed Donald to develop his belief in the importance of the Methodist tradition was a first-year course on English Methodism. This involved fourteen lectures in which the development of Methodism was carefully outlined. At each stage Methodism was set in its wider religious and societal context. Donald acknowledged in his lectures on John Wesley that Wesley was in some ways 'the despair of both the descriptive historian and the systematic theologian', and he suggested that part of John Wesley's great significance was the way in which different elements of his character, life and teaching appealed to vastly different people. In this sense the evangelical experience that shaped Wesley was not narrow. Linked to this, Donald suggested that Methodism was 'a revival of religious experience' rather than a doctrinal movement, although he also said that the defence of the doctrine was seen as essential to the spread of the experience. It is significant that some evangelical students who hoped that Donald might give them an 'easy ride' were soon disappointed. Leo Osborn, at that time a Bristol student, later minister of Cullercoats Methodist Church and then Chair of the Newcastle upon Tyne District, recalls the way in which Donald critiqued a 'good sound evangelical' essay that Osborn submitted.[9]

Donald also taught courses at Wesley on mission, worship, the person and work of Christ, and the ministry in modern Methodism. The course on worship dealt with the different traditions in worship, and Donald also gave guidance to students on how to lead worship in different settings. His thinking on worship was published in 1975 as *God in the Gallery*.[10] Donald's range of teaching shows the desire he had throughout his ministry to connect theology, history and contemporary practice. To some extent this meant that Donald never specialised in a particular area and perhaps as a result he did not produce a book which could be reckoned to be a significant contribution to scholarship. His view of his role as a college tutor was that he was able to help in more practically orientated ways with ministerial development, although he was determined that this should always happen through biblical and theological reflection. The course he offered on the ministry in modern Methodism, for example, was a very practical third-year course. It looked at the various rules, relationships and tasks of Methodist ministers. It took as background the Methodist Conference definitions of ministry, but also the rapidly changing society, the growing awareness of the ministries of the whole people of God, and the diverse convictions, abilities and skills of the ministers themselves. The minister was seen as a leader, a representative, a pastor, a missioner, a theologian, an administrator, a colleague, a Christian and a human being. The course was not simply a 'how-to' course for those about to enter ministry; it had strong theological and historical undergirding.

---

[9] Osborn, 'Donald English – Pastor', p. 18.
[10] D. English, *God in the Gallery* (London: Epworth Press, 1975).

One of Donald's most imaginative pieces of work while he was in Bristol was his initiation of field studies. This part of the training meant that a whole year's intake of students would go away for ten days or a fortnight to study the social context and church programme of particular local Methodist congregations. Donald himself would lead the team, prepare each visit with great care, and open up contacts with local schools, social service agencies, hospitals, the police and various community leaders. There would then follow a careful analysis of the church's situation in that town and discussion with the minister, church leaders and members about appropriate strategies for mission. These field studies included places like Swindon and Cheltenham, as well as Bristol. If the local people through these contacts and through exploring the need for mission in their area wanted further help, then the college might offer them Donald and the team to come on mission some months later. Students were always keen to go on field trips and missions because Donald did not just make the arrangements – he was the leader of the group. He took a full part with the students in the field study situations.

In this way and in other ways Donald kept in close contact with Methodist circuit life on the ground. He was keen not to get out of touch with new developments in the Methodist denomination. One such development in this period was that Methodism decided to accept women as presbyters. Initially, all the women accepted (eighteen) were sent to Bristol for training. Some were senior deaconesses who had done twenty years or more of pastoral work. Donald, with his colleagues, was committed to this fresh move for Methodism in the area of ministry. But Donald was not simply one who reacted to new developments. As part of Donald's wider contribution to Christian mission, he took preaching appointments across the country. He was becoming better known to the wider Methodist and non-Methodist

Christian community and was in increasing demand around the country as a speaker. There were some who criticised what they saw as his frequent absences from the college. However, in his mind, there was the need for a constant integration between colleges and the churches. Also, Donald was conscious of the gifts he believed God had entrusted to him, and he was anxious to use those gifts as widely and effectively as possible.

An example of Donald's concern as a theological teacher to be relevant to the actual situations faced by the churches is a paper he gave a Wesley College old students' refresher course held at Easter 1974. This was on the issue of the charismatic movement in the Methodist Church. The material in this lecture was used in other addresses subsequently. Donald suggested that in a church dominated by concern for ecumenical activity the fact that charismatics were breaking down denominational and confessional boundaries, albeit in a limited area, was worthy of attention. Also, he noted that the Methodist Conference had requested the denomination's Faith and Order Committee to produce advice on the movement and that leaders of the movement had themselves requested comment and further discussion. In November 1974 Donald drafted the 'Faith and Order' report.[11] He had an increasing personal interest in the issue through the experiences of members of his congregation, through his personal friendship with most of the movement's leaders in Methodism and through his student involvement. Having outlined the history of Pentecostalism and the charismatic movement, Donald suggested that on the hotly disputed issue of speaking in tongues as initial evidence of baptism in the Spirit, the impression he had was that tongues as initial evidence was less and less the view

---

[11] 'Proposed Report to the Conference on the Charismatic Movement', Faith and Order Committee, Ref. 1974/15, D. English, 9/11/74.

among charismatics within Methodism. He believed that the understanding of the activity of the Spirit within Methodist charismatic circles was finding its place alongside teaching and experiences that were typical of Methodism.

Donald then asked: how naturally does charismatic teaching find a home in Methodism? In terms of the teaching and practice of John Wesley and of the Methodist Revival as a whole, he suggested, there was not much commendatory teaching or record of charismatic activity. Wesley modified an earlier view and came to believe that the gifts present in the early church were withdrawn because of unbelief and disobedience. There were ways, however, Donald argued, in which charismatics could claim a very close link between Methodism and their experience. There was a direct link between Wesley's teaching on sanctification and the beginnings of the Pentecostal movement via the nineteenth-century Holiness Movements. There was also Wesley's stress upon a second experience and Wesley's teaching about the importance of evidences to substantiate any claim to religious experience. Other points mentioned in this paper by Donald were Wesley's optimism of grace, with its glad openness to all that God had for the believer and a refusal to limit the promises of God or their fulfilment in human life; Wesley's concern for the witness of the Spirit, personally experienced; and the way in which Wesley emphasised the area of personal salvation, albeit with practical, corporate and social outworking. At the same time, Donald noted that there were elements in Wesley's teaching that would be an obstacle to some forms of charismatic emphasis: his great stress upon reason, for example. Donald's concern was to give a balanced assessment but to show that this important new movement had a place within Methodist life. At the end of this paper, Donald set out some characteristically judicious conclusions:

1. He saw it as important that Methodist ministers respond – personally in their study and publicly where possible – to the charismatic leaders' openness to further examination and comment on the biblical and theological bases on which the movement stood.

2. He advocated assessment being offered from a basis of knowledge and not ignorance or prejudice; and where possible from first-hand knowledge.

3. He encouraged ministers to be ready to deal with pastoral issues thrown up by the presence of members of the movement in congregations. This would involve knowing what they were talking about, being able to relate sympathetically to them, and having an atmosphere of mutual tolerance within the life of the church as a whole.

4. Finally he pondered on whether the whole movement might be a judgement upon the inadequacy of some Methodist (and perhaps other) teaching, particularly about the potential of the Christian life. It could well be, he suggested, that much of what the baptism in the Spirit brought to charismatics was what all Christians should know from the beginning of their Christian experience, and that difficulties in accepting it later stemmed from the fact that it was out of its proper phase in the Christian life.

Donald believed that conservative evangelicals, including his students, faced particular challenges in a time of social and spiritual change. The idea of being 'conservative' could be equated with opposition to any changes. In a paper produced in 1975, Donald took up this topic.[12] He recognised the concern that the evangelical approach (he said that he preferred not to add 'conservative') to the spiritual life might be too directive and restrictive. He affirmed, however, that he

[12] D. English, 'Conservative Evangelicals in Methodist Ministry', October 1975. Unpublished.

had not found it to be so. In connection specifically with pastoral ministry, Donald suggested that Jesus began where people were, with endless openness and concern, and that this was the model for the evangelical minister. He highlighted also the biblical emphasis on the influence upon people of environment and heredity. On the other hand, there was the biblical insistence on people accepting responsibility for their actions. He saw these twin foci as essential in pastoralia. He also found himself, as he put it, 'very much prepared by the biblical evangelical view to look over the whole field of psychology, psychiatry and psychotherapy'. In Donald's mind there was no need for evangelicals to rule out the contribution from these fields of knowledge, but neither should they be accepted uncritically.

Throughout his years of teaching at Wesley, Donald English was not simply someone whom students knew only at a distance as a classroom lecturer. Those who knew him stress his approachability. His personal relationships with the students were regarded by John A. Newton as being excellent. Graham Evans recalls the way in which Donald was:

> willing to spend time to help me come to terms with the critical comments which were being made about the Scriptures. We sat in his study and he talked of the life changing power of the Scriptures (and the one they pointed to) and the way that the Holy Spirit inspired the writers and still inspires both the preacher and congregation. It was the basis of my growing confidence in the Bible.

Bob Kitching speaks about the enthusiasm with which Donald and Bertha often opened their home to students. These students valued such friendship and came to know Bertha and the two boys, Richard and Paul, who by the late 1970s were both in their teens.

During the later 1970s Donald was acutely aware that traditional views of ministry were changing and that, as a theological teacher and a person involved in preparing students for ministry, this must be an area he had to tackle. In 1978 he formulated a fourfold view of ministry: vocational, charismatic, functional and representative.[13] Under vocational he included the awareness on the part of a person that he or she had been called and that this had been confirmed by others. This call had to be nourished and developed in ministry. The second element, the charismatic, had to do with gifts, and Donald suggested that 'there may be a larger number of gifts which enable people to be ordained ministers than the traditional ones of being able to preach, visit, conduct meetings, and give leadership to the life of the church'. On the other hand, Donald resisted the idea of a minister who had all kinds of gifts. A third way of looking at ministry was to see it as a job to be done. Donald believed that there was a special function in ministry apart from the functions performed, and he knew that most of the functions normally applied to ordained ministry were by this stage also being carried out by lay people. But there was special overall function for the ordained minister. The lay calling was to undertake limited functions. Finally the representative element involved a recognition that ministers had offered themselves in a particular way, had been authorised in a particular way, and therefore represented the church as no one else did. It was this high concept of ministry that Donald held out to his students.

Two years later, in January 1980, he reflected again, to a Methodist study group, on ministry, considering at greater depth the breakdown of the old division between lay and ordained ministry and the possible tensions that this change

---

[13] D. English, 'Notes on Ministry and Ordination', 1978. Unpublished.

had caused. There was hardly any area in the ordained minister's activities which had not been entered by lay people
equally or better trained to do so. This, he suggested, operated at the level of preaching, conducting worship, counselling, visiting, administration, and even in sharing the
administration of the sacraments. He believed it was therefore more and more difficult to define a minister's role
simply in terms of his doing what lay people do not do. For
him this opened up the possibility of debate about tension
and relationships. He looked at tensions in ecumenical relationships, over spirituality and worship, and in the wider
social and religious milieu, and he argued that Methodists
ought to be able to handle tension, since John Wesley
seemed to have been a past master of the art.

In seeking to understand the role of tensions in ministry,
Donald made the fascinating suggestion that the major contribution of John Wesley to the theological thinking of the
Christian church was not primarily in the matter of the
doctrines often associated with him – particularly assurance
and perfect love – but in his capacity to carry tension within
his theological system. Those who wanted something
neater and simpler, Donald believed, often ended up by
being unrelated to the variety and breadth of human life.
But Wesley could handle tension between justification by
grace through faith and the affirmation that the works we
do are our works. Wesley was willing to affirm a perfect
love that allowed for mistakes and errors and which needed
to grow. In Wesley's thinking a person's assurance did not
remove the possibility of falling away. Wesley was able to
include crises and processes within the normal Christian
experience. Making application to contemporary ministry,
Donald surveyed the various models for handling tension:
comprehensive agreement, selective agreement, comple-
mentarity and convergence. For Donald, the model of
convergence meant drawing from different sources. This

was increasingly his own vision in ministry. 'The result', he said, 'is mobile, uncertain, patchy, sometimes tempestuous, but certainly exciting and demanding.'[14] It was a theme to which he would often return.

What was vital for Donald, and what summed up the functions that he spoke about in lectures in the 1970s,[15] was the incarnational principle. He believed that for a minister to communicate properly he or she had to engage deeply with people. Ministers had to seek to understand how it was to be the other person if they were to achieve anything in a loving relationship with him or her. He insisted that a minister must respect the capacity of the other person in terms of what he or she was able to receive and understand. Too often, Donald suggested, a clever minister demonstrated intellectual ability, and destroyed the faith of some of the hearers. On what then was a healthy ministry built? There must be recognition of the significant sources of authority that were being used. In this John Wesley was seen by Donald as a very good guide. On the pattern of the 'mobile', Wesley saw the Bible as central. Circulating around it were reason, tradition and experience. The whole thing, said Donald, *was* mobile, which meant that Wesley looked at the Bible through experience, tradition and reason, but also allowed the Bible to judge experience, tradition and reason. For Donald this was a crucial insight. Wesley himself, Donald remarked, was mobile. He could choose the vantage point from which he viewed biblical material, often according to the question he was asking. Donald reminded Methodist ministers that they were not only to proclaim the gospel; they were to live by it. He concluded: 'As the Elizabethan Bishop Weston said, it is

[14] D. English, 'The Experience of Tension in Theological and Ecclesiastical Relationships', January 1980. Unpublished.

[15] Notes entitled, 'Ministry in Modern Methodism', used in the 1970s.

necessary for us to be good shepherds that we be good sheep.'

* * * * *

In this chapter we have looked especially at some of the things that Donald English was saying about ministry during his time as a theological teacher. He was also under-taking an increasing amount of writing, however, even if his writing was largely in the form of pamphlets and small books rather than major works.[16] His publications, though important, never quite made the same impact as his speaking ministry, and in any case his more significant books were not written until a later stage in his ministry. Never-theless we see in his writing great perceptiveness, lucidity and a capacity to make profound truths and complex theo-logical problems accessible to ordinary readers. As Richard Andrew, Director of the York Institute for Community Theology, has pointed out, Donald was a writer with an enormous respect for learning.[17] He was also a writer with evangelical passion. Yet he never sought to be an evangeli-cal in isolation from the broad streams of Christian faith nor of the contemporary world. There is much to admire throughout Donald's writings, which on the whole, says Andrew, were aimed at popular consumption – though this is not to denigrate his achievements. He was capable of works of scholarship as well, but always committed to making scholarship palatable to ordinary readers. It is this accessibility in his writings that make some think that they are less profound than they are in reality.

Perhaps Donald's most significant book during his years as a theological college tutor was *God in the Gallery*, a book

---

[16] See Appendix 2 for a full list of publications by Donald English.
[17] R.M. Andrew, 'Donald English – the Writer' in Abbott (ed.), *Donald English*, pp. 35–7.

that gives a valuable insight into his thinking about worship and preaching. Important later publications include *The Meaning of the Warmed Heart* (which was translated into no less than twenty-five languages for use throughout World Methodism), his IVP commentary *The Message of Mark*, and the booklet *Into the 21st Century*. The pinnacle of his achievements as a writer, however, in the view of Richard Andrew – a view shared by many others – is found in *An Evangelical Theology of Preaching*, several chapters of which began life as lectures at Asbury Theological Seminary in the USA. It is a book that brings together the fruit of a life-time's reflection on the nature and context of preaching by one who spoke with a rare authority upon these matters. Donald's distinctive contribution as a writer, but especially as a teacher, lay in his ability to read intellectual and spiritual currents in the light of the historical evangelical Methodist tradition and to translate their implications for mission and ministry into a form that could be widely understood. That, surely, is the mark of a theological teacher of true ability.

6

Methodist Leader

Donald English was one of the outstanding Methodist denominational leaders of the later twentieth century. He had the distinction of being President of the Methodist Conference in 1978 and again in 1990, the only person to be elected President twice since Methodist union in 1932. From 1982 until his retirement in 1995 he served as General Secretary of the Methodist Home Mission Division. In wider British life there were a number of state occasions where he had a prominent role. He was lunching with the Queen when his second term as President of the Methodist Conference was announced in the Conference. His influence was also felt in other circles. He led Bible studies for Members of Parliament and for a group in the House of Lords, addressed High Court judges and barristers and broadcast regularly on the radio, a medium he greatly enjoyed. He was especially known for his incisive 'Thought for the Day' talks on the BBC Radio Four *Today* programme. In all these spheres his desire was to be an effective representative of the Christian faith, particularly bringing a distinctive Methodist witness.

Although his gifts were becoming increasingly recognised by the Connexion as a whole throughout the 1970s, it was among his fellow Methodist evangelicals that Donald's leadership abilities were first exercised and acknowledged.

His emergence as an evangelical leader took place at a time when many Methodists were deeply suspicious of any 'party' groups within the church, whether evangelical or radical, and those who held views that were considered to be on the theological extremes were aware of this suspicion. To some extent, as David Bebbington argues, the radical theology that came to the fore in wider church life in Britain in the 1960s – some of it characterised by the promotion of the idea of the 'death of God' – strengthened the evangelical position. Conservative evangelicals were not slow to denounce what they saw as departures from orthodoxy.[1] Many within Methodism's leadership, however, wanted to avoid a destructive polarisation. Accordingly, the President of Conference for 1970 to 1971, Rupert E. Davies, offered himself as a theological catalyst to the various groups that existed in Methodism, and encouraged evangelicals among others to make a positive theological contribution within the denomination. This seemed to offer an opportunity for evangelical engagement.

Donald English took the initiative in responding to this by calling a three-day conference of Methodist evangelicals at Cliff College in November 1970. It was out of this that the organisation Conservative Evangelicals in Methodism (CEIM) was born, although it was unlikely that this was quite the sort of response the President had in mind. The conference brought together forty-four Methodist ministers, two deaconesses and nine lay men and women representing a variety of ages, experience and background, and Donald himself chose the names and invited them. He particularly wanted people from different parts of the country. Those who came were united by an urgent concern about the discouragement and isolation felt by some conservative evangelicals within Methodism. Martin Turner describes

---

[1] Bebbington, *Evangelicalism in Modern Britain*, p. 255.

how he and other evangelicals were thrilled by Donald's vision.[2] They wanted to find ways of expressing the conservative evangelical position. After three days of discussion and prayer at Cliff it was the overwhelming conviction of the conference that an association should be formed to continue what had been started. A committee of seven people was appointed, with Howard Belben, the Principal of Cliff College, as Chair, and with the committee members including Donald and the Methodist historian Arthur Skevington Wood.[3] Within a few months CEIM had come into being, affiliated to the Evangelical Alliance and comprising Methodist ministers and lay people all over Britain, with the avowed purpose of making the evangelical voice more clearly heard within Methodist life.

There was an existing organisation that brought together evangelicals in Methodism, the Methodist Revival Fellowship (MRF), and two decades later the MRF and CEIM would combine to form one organisation, Headway. The MRF had as its aim the bringing together of Methodists 'who are really concerned that the Methodist Church should, under the hand of God, fulfil its historic mission, and who are longing for an outpouring of the Holy Spirit upon the Churches'. But for several years before 1970 the MRF Committee (of which Donald had been a member) had had in mind the creation of 'an evangelical ginger-group within the denomination to consider theological issues and then judge evangelical strategy'.[4] In order to expand the influence of CEIM, those present at the November 1970 conference offered the names of others they knew in Methodism who took the conservative evangelical point of view. This, said

[2] M. Turner, 'Donald English – Mentor' in Abbott (ed.), *Donald English*, p. 32.

[3] 'Conservative Evangelicals in Methodism', draft of introductory letter, 1970.

[4] 'If I will … what is that to thee?', MRF briefing paper, 1971.

Donald English to Leslie Davison (the then General Secretary of the Home Mission Department) in December 1970, showed that the representation of conservative evangelicals in Methodism was larger than was often recognised.

Conservative evangelicals, Donald believed, had not tried to make their presence felt connexionally. They had, rather, tended to concentrate on preaching and pastoral work, not on political and ecclesiastical areas of Methodist life. Donald thought that, although from some points of view this had been commendable, it was in fact a mistake.[5] But was evangelical influence on Methodist ecclesiastical life a realistic goal? Some thought not. Roland Lamb wrote to Donald in December 1970 to argue against continuing within Methodism. Lamb had himself left the denomination by this time and was General Secretary of the British Evangelical Council. Lamb reminded Donald of their days in Leicester. He now saw their paths as very far apart, although Donald himself recalled Lamb as one of his teachers in those formative years.[6] Evangelicals in the later 1960s had divided sharply over the question of separation from those who held non-evangelical theological positions. Donald's commitment was to denominational involvement.

From 1974 onwards Donald was Chair of CEIM. In the October 1974 issue of the *CEIM Newsletter* he emphasised the aims of CEIM: to explore the implications of the evangelical understanding of the Christian faith and to play a full part within Methodism, so that the evangelical position might be properly expressed and understood.[7] By this time it was felt that the work of CEIM was being widely appreciated. Donald was determined that the movement should seek to avoid purely devotional and inspirational material, which he saw as being very adequately provided by magazines like

[5] D. English to Revd Dr Leslie Davison, 7 December 1970.
[6] R. Lamb to D. English, 16 December 1970.
[7] *CEIM Newsletter*, 12 October 1974, p. 7.

Sound of Revival and *Dunamis*. He also wished to maintain a watchful attitude towards developments within Methodism and, where possible, to make comments and present material. This was a particularly acute need in 1974, as a number of Methodists were deeply concerned about a Methodist textbook for local preachers that had been published, entitled *Doing Theology*. In March 1974 one Methodist minister, Victor Budgen from Milnrow, Rochdale, wrote to Donald to say that he had resigned from Methodist ministry, his resignation being precipitated by the theological pluralism expressed in *Doing Theology*. Some evangelical ministers were experiencing hostility in circuit life. Donald replied to Budgen to express sympathy and sadness, but also pointed out that as a result of criticisms that he and another CEIM committee member, David Sharp, had made of *Doing Theology*, another book would be produced which would 'state categorically the traditional biblical doctrine of the Christian faith'. Both books would be used for the Methodist local preachers' course.[8]

In the mid-1970s Donald English was being looked to as one who could keep conservative evangelicals within Methodism and there were hopes also on the part of evangelicals that he would improve the climate for their work. But every month, it seemed, there was news of people leaving Methodism, mainly lay people. When Budgen resigned, for example, he had been joined by forty lay people. In writing to such people, as Donald did on occasions with the encouragement of Kenneth Greet, Secretary of Conference, Donald stressed the positive signs within Methodism, such as the way the charismatic movement was bringing a fair number of Methodists back to a position of basic confidence in the Bible. On the other hand, writing to Kenneth Greet, Donald bluntly stated his view that the publishing of *Doing Theology* had

---

[8] V. Budgen to D. English, 8 March 1974; D. English to V. Budgen, 15 March 1974.

been a mistake, and that for every person who was resigning from Methodism there were many others who felt that the theology of the book had made them feel less at home in Methodism than they had before.[9] At this point CEIM had about 400 members. In the light of the growth of the charismatic movement, a day conference was held in 1974, which drew together CEIM members, representatives of the much larger MRF and charismatic leaders. The result was perceived to be greater understanding and recognition of common ground.[10]

Against this background, Donald delivered an important CEIM paper in October 1975 on 'A Conservative Evangelical in Methodism'. He argued that the term 'conservative evangelical' was necessary. He preferred the description 'Christian', but considered that it was rather presumptuous simply to describe one's theological position as 'Christian': it ignored others' viewpoints and appeared to canonise one's own. Regarding the term 'evangelical Christian', without 'conservative', he suggested that in some Protestant traditions this simply meant 'non-Catholic'. Thus he saw 'conservative evangelical Christians' as 'saddled with' that term since clarity, integrity and mutual exploration required some recognition of the fact of differing viewpoints, for example over Scripture. The 'conservative' part of the title stemmed largely from a view of the Bible, but this was by no means the sole factor that gave conservative evangelicals their identity. In this address, Donald sought to define the essence of what it was to be evangelical. He cited Karl Barth, who in his *Evangelical Theology* argued that evangelical theology is about God as revealed in his deeds; God supremely revealed in the gospel through the Word; and God as being with humankind. But Donald's main reliance

---

[9] D. English to W. and K. Adlum, 3 April 1974; D. English to K. Greet, 3 April 1974; D. English to J. Hall, 15 May 1974.

[10] Minutes of Annual General Meeting of CEIM, 1 July 1974.

was on the evangelical Anglican leader John Stott. To be evangelical, for Stott, meant being committed to theology, the Bible, the apostolic faith and fundamental doctrines.[11] Donald affirmed these points, arguing for theological convictions related to the content of the gospel, though he did not see these as being static. The recent Lausanne Congress and Covenant of 1975, which emphasised the social and political implications of the gospel, was for him a good example of how biblical study could revise evangelical presuppositions.[12]

During this same period Donald observed what he saw as 'the renewal of interest in three areas of the Christian life which have always been close to the heart of evangelicals'. These were spirituality, Bible study and evangelism. On spirituality, he considered it would be a great pity if evangelicals within Methodism were not engaged in debates about this matter, either because they assumed that the daily quiet time and weekly worship and fellowship were enough, or because many who were interested seemed to be on the Catholic wing of the church. He suggested that there was a need for evangelicals to ask whether the traditional methods of devotion were still adequate. The importance of silence and of meditation were two topics that he proposed as worthy of attention. Concerning Bible study, Donald welcomed a renewed interest in such study among Methodists (and others) who were tired of social gatherings which passed for class meetings or fellowship groups. Here again, he suggested that evangelicals would need to ask whether inherited methods of group Bible study were adequate. The same was true, he believed, about evangelism. Evangelicals could humbly claim to have gone on believing in and

[11] J. Stott, *Christ the Controversialist* (London: Tyndale, 1970), p. 27 ff.

[12] D. English, 'A Conservative Evangelical in the Methodist Ministry', October 1975. Unpublished.

practising evangelism throughout 'the barren years of the 1960s' when they were being told that the God they were proclaiming was dead. However, they should still ask whether existing ways remained effective and relevant.[13]

As well as being an advocate of evangelical convictions, Donald was someone who was seen (especially in the later 1970s) as provoking evangelicals within Methodism to look critically at their lives. He noted in 1975 that there had been a tendency on the part of conservative evangelicals to resist all modern forms of biblical criticism as being opposed to the evangelical view of Scripture, and he welcomed the wider viewpoint that was emerging, commending the example of the Methodist New Testament scholar Howard Marshall at the University of Aberdeen. Donald also advocated a positive attitude to the whole field of psychology, psychiatry and psychotherapy in relation to pastoralia. He argued that evangelicals had much to learn from others, instancing theological radicals with their political and social involvement, and Catholics who promoted sacramental views. Donald's belief was that evangelicals should not be afraid of testing their positions. He saw it as regrettable when evangelical concern for simplicity turned into naïveté; when positive faith meant being negative about rational enquiry; when a high evaluation of spiritual experience and growth created neglect of necessary ecclesiastical structures; when the doctrine of redemption limited an understanding of creation; and when concern for the individual left little room for influencing society. None the less, Donald insisted that none of these tendencies was inevitable. For him, biblical faith was radical, and he quoted John Wesley: 'If I become a heretic I become so by reading the Bible!'[14]

---

[13] Notes in personal papers, 1975.

[14] D. English, 'A Conservative Evangelical in the Methodist Ministry', October 1975. Unpublished.

His creative concerns meant that Donald was coming more and more to the attention of mainstream Methodism. It was this that led to his being elected President of Conference in 1978. He was then forty-seven, one of the three youngest presidents in Methodist history. His presidential address did not probe so deeply as some of his other reflections, but he spoke helpfully about the response of the church to massive social change, theological exploration, liturgical groups and charismatic experience. Donald affirmed the growing confidence about proclaiming the Christian good news and the increasing improvement at informal levels of relationships between Christians. He declared: 'We have lots of good and moving stories to tell. Why do we not tell them?' Donald used Psalm 130, which had so deeply affected John Wesley on 24 May 1738, the day of his Aldersgate Street experience, when he heard the anthem from the Psalm, including the words 'O Israel, hope in the Lord'. Donald outlined aspects of hope and of pilgrimage.[15] During his ensuing presidential year Donald's stated ambition was to emphasise the relevance of biblical teaching to twentieth-century life and especially to young people. He asked for youth rallies to be held wherever he travelled.

Donald's continuing commitment to both CEIM and the MRF was evident during his presidential year. As Chair of CEIM he addressed the 1978 conference at Cliff College. Giving the major address of the weekend, he said that within Methodism evangelism was a major topic of concern, preaching was being taken with increasing seriousness and a more positive note of faith and commitment was evident in church life. Another positive feature was the openness to evangelical contributions to moral and ethical debates.

---

[15] D. English, Presidential Address, 1978; *Methodist Recorder*, 20 July 1978, pp. 24–6.

'A right to be heard', said Donald, 'is earned by the quality of our love for others.' However, he saw the church's record on evangelism as 'pathetic', and criticised the slogan 'Every Christian an Evangelist', since, although all were witnesses, not all were evangelists. Donald also spoke to 300 people at the annual Prayer Conference of the MRF held at The Hayes conference centre, Swanwick, Derbyshire. All available places for this weekend were fully booked within three days of the conference being announced, and many applications had to be refused. Donald brought a devotional address on the Sunday morning.[16] He was by now the undoubted leader of evangelicals in Methodism.

During his period as Conference President, Donald began to send out a prayer letter to supporters around the country, and he continued this practice after his presidency. The letters were typed and distributed by Margaret Allwood, a member of Farnsfield Methodist Church, near Mansfield, and a local preacher in her circuit. These letters included personal news, updates and prayer requests. Some CEIM and MRF members, in the light of the experience of praying in this way for Donald, requested that prayer news of this kind should be produced officially by or for every President/Vice-President of Conference. Ron Abbott, as Secretary of the MRF, wrote to Donald about this and took up his recommendation to seek to implement this idea through a memorial to Conference. The suggestion was taken up. A presidential prayer card, published annually by the Methodist Publishing House, was the result.

On the retirement of George Sails in 1982, Donald was appointed as General Secretary of the Home Mission Division of the Methodist Church. During his presidential year his travels had enabled him to get to know the denomination even better, and his long-held commitment to mission and

---

[16] *Methodist Recorder*, 9 November 1978, p. 8.

his track record in evangelism equipped him well for this Divisional post. Peter Sutcliffe, who succeeded Donald as General Secretary when he retired, recalls having been in the Methodist Conference Office in 1980 when the Secretary of Conference, Kenneth Greet, was sounding out opinions on who should be appointed to the Home Mission secretary-ship. Derek Farrow, General Secretary of the Finance Division, declared himself 'a Donald English man', saying 'it would be good for us to have someone with a known theological position in that office'. Sutcliffe observed, 'It would not do justice to Donald to put a label on him, though he was known for his sound evangelical ministry. Yet within the Division the spectrum was wide, and we were all encouraged to make our contribution.'

David Bridge was already on the staff of the Division when Donald became General Secretary, and describes how he operated. Donald believed that he had a special responsi-bility for Methodist mission and that he had been granted gifts for his task. This could, said David Bridge, sometimes make working with him difficult. As an example of day-to-day problems, on one occasion Bridge returned to the office after a day away and found that Donald had 'borrowed' his secretary, with the result that his own work was delayed. Bridge continues: 'When I confronted Donald with this he was deeply distressed. I just do not think it occurred to him that other colleagues might have important work in hand also. I do not write this as a criticism as it is probable that Donald's work had higher priority in the Kingdom. It was just that few of us were saintly enough to realise this at the time.' Donald had a very clear sense of his vocation, which was to lead the church in mission. His method was to lead the Division from the front. He did almost all the talking at Conference, for example – and in David Bridge's view this was probably justified, since he did it better than anyone else.

Donald's deep loyalty to his staff could sometimes go awry. One example of this was precipitated by a prank. A Superintendent wrote an angry letter to Donald saying that a circuit colleague of his had been asked by David Bridge to write a piece for the *Home Mission Review* on the theme of the consequences for faith of the discovery of life on other planets. The Superintendent, not surprisingly, thought the idea was preposterous. Donald wrote a long reply to the Superintendent in question, at least a page and a half, to say that though he had no knowledge of the matter he felt sure that David Bridge would have a good reason for the request, and he went on to suggest some possible implications for the faith of the discovery of intelligent life elsewhere in the universe. As an expression of loyalty to Bridge, the letter was exemplary. However, had Donald thought to walk down the corridor to talk to David Bridge, he would have discovered that David had not solicited an article on that theme from anyone and that the whole thing sprang from a hoax. But such lapses on Donald's part were unusual. His colleagues appreciated the way he sought to give a sense of importance and value to the specific work done by everybody within the Division and brought the best out of each member of his team by believing in them, trusting them and encouraging them.

Coupled with his strong leadership, Donald was instinctively a team builder and a team player – how could a footballer be otherwise? Margaret Parker, who was elected Vice-President of Conference for 1998 to 1999, and who spent many years as a Conference representative and a member of committees, has spoken in positive terms of Donald's effective leadership in this respect.[17] His affirmation of different viewpoints held together as a team the theologically diverse staff of the Home Mission Division.

[17] M. Parker, 'Donald English – Statesman' in Abbott (ed.), *Donald English*, pp. 26–8.

Increasingly, during his years at Home Mission, Donald devolved responsibility for various areas of mission work to members of the wider 'field staff', encouraging them (as the tribute written in 1994 at the end of his term of service put it) 'to develop their own style, prepare their own budgets, and dream their own dreams'. It was recognised that Donald built up a strong sense of fellowship within the Division through his skilful leadership of staff meetings and through bringing together – as he had done in his periods as a member of various college staff teams – people of differing views, helping them to value and affirm each other. Donald acted with considerable astuteness when dealing with the challenges of the office context. He could be very firm with members of the team whose work was below standard, and was keen to set targets and to have staff appraisal, but he was known to combine firmness with graciousness. He always took a personal and not simply a professional interest in junior and senior members of staff alike.

As an example of Donald's method of delegation at work, when he realised that Peter Sutcliffe, the London Mission Secretary at the Division, was skilled with figures, Donald quickly delegated to him the responsibility of overseeing the grant aid programme. Says Sutcliffe:

> Hitherto, this had been the prerogative of the General Secretary, perhaps on the thesis that money equalled authority. Donald didn't need that. In the first year we formulated our recommendations to the Divisional Board together. Thereafter he was content to leave the programme in my hands knowing that he was there if I needed him. I also had the theory that he thought saying 'No' might come easier to a Yorkshireman than to one of his kindly disposition!

It was inevitable that Donald's Home Mission responsibilities would involve a great number of committees. Some people viewed committee work as a burdensome chore, but for Donald it was a corporate way of getting things done effectively. Kenneth Greet recalls that Donald always had a pen in his hand and was constantly taking notes, even of the most mundane discussions, which Greet suggests was part of the secret of his grasp of every issue that came up. He had the striking ability to make committees productive and to imbue them with a sense of vision and purpose, so that the agenda item 'Date of the next meeting' became one to which members actually looked forward. On some committees he served in an *ex officio* capacity. He was invited on to others because of his abilities and standing. He chaired the Cliff College Committee, for instance, and played an important part in ensuring that the college's historic stance and its strong mission emphasis was not only preserved but brought more fully into the life of the Connexion. He was Chair of the governors for Southlands College and played a significant part in its developing links with the Roehampton Institute and its eventual recognition as a constituent college within the University of Surrey.

Although Methodism was his primary concern, Donald's leadership within ecclesiastical circles reached further. It was largely on his initiative that colleagues with mission responsibilities in other denominations were brought together in what became the Heads of Mission Meeting (the precursor of the Churches Together in England Group for Evangelisation), which met in his office and which he chaired. Never one simply to keep things ticking over, Donald was responsible for other important initiatives. A particularly significant one was the recognition of the special gifts that Rob Frost had in evangelism and the secur-ing of a non-circuit Methodist appointment that would enable him to use those gifts within the Connexion. This led to the beginnings of events like Easter People (Donald gave the Bible readings at the very first one in 1988). Rob Frost's

Donald's parents,
Robert and Ena English

Donald with his parents

Consett Grammar School Football XI, 1947.
Donald – back row, second from the right

Donald (front row left) as a
member of the First Aid team
in the Tenth Consett
Company, North-West
Durham Boys Brigade of the

Graduate, University
College, Leicester

Leicester Christian Union, Summer 1957.
Donald fifth from the left, front row

Donald (third from right, front row) as a
student at Wesley House, Cambridge

Donald as a newly-
ordained minister

Donald and Bertha's wedding, 1962

Donald and Bertha before
taking part in the Royal
Wedding, 1986

Donald, Bertha and their dog, Abi,
at Shipton-under-Wychwood, the
year after Donald's retirement

Donald at Trinity College, Umuahia,
Nigeria, November 1974

The Tutorial Staff at Wesley College, Bristol.
Left to right: Ivor Jones, Donald English,
John Newton, Raymond George, Peter Stephens,
Sybil Hodge, Kenneth Wilson

Donald at a civic reception in Consett, 1978, during his presidency of the Methodist Conference

Donald speaking at the Southern Asia Bishops' Retreat, New Delhi, India, 1980

World Methodist Council Officers, 1991

Meeting the Pope

In conversation with Margaret Thatcher

Donald being awarded his CBE, 1996

Outside
Buckingham
Palace

work has now developed into 'Share Jesus International', a mission organisation serving not only Methodism, but all the major denominations in England.

Another aspect of the leadership that Donald offered Methodism as part of his calling to Home Mission was through the initiatives 'Mission Alongside the Poor' and 'Sharing in God's Mission'. Donald introduced to Conference in 1983 the report from the President's Council on 'Mission Alongside the Poor', which incorporated material from the divisions of Home Mission, Ministries and Social Responsibility. Donald said that Methodism took 'very seriously indeed the vital importance of continuing a Methodist presence in some areas of our land where life is hard now and likely to get harder'. There was commitment to closer identification with the poor and a special fund was to be set up to raise £1 million over five years.[18] Donald recognised the complexities of the issues, and his book *Sharing in God's Mission* offered a profound theological synthesis of evangelism, social care and the struggle for justice. This book became one of Methodism's basic documents. Subsequently in his *Into the 21st Century* he offered a visionary response to the kind of world that the church was likely to be facing, and examined the present state of the church. It was a book he had planned to expand.

During the whole of his time at the Home Mission Division Donald was faithfully and ably assisted by his PA, Irene Bower. She writes:

> Each morning Donald's desk had various piles of papers [on it] and he knew what was in each pile. Each evening before he left the office the papers were put away and the desk was left clear and tidy. On one occasion I went to meet him in a café at a London station when he had an hour to spare between trains.

---

[18] *Methodist Recorder*, 7 July 1983, p. 10.

He had been away for several days and had prepared some work, and we could discuss what had arrived in the post during his absence. When I arrived Donald was already there, seated at the table with a pot of tea, and there was his work before him, all in neat piles. It was just like walking into his office!

Irene always did her best to protect Donald from unwanted pressures, but it was often a losing battle. 'If Donald had a fault', she writes:

it was trying to meet all the demands on his time. However busy he was, his door was open to all. He gave sound advice and therefore a queue formed at his door ... He was working from 9.00am to 9.00pm or more for five days a week and preaching and speaking most weekends, but when I suggested he ought to look at his lifestyle I lost the argument. He retorted straight away 'But I am a preacher!'

*   *   *   *   *

In 1990 Donald became President of the Conference for the second time. There were those who were critical of his decision to allow his name to go forward again, some seeing it as power seeking and others feeling that in principle nobody should ever serve more than once. Letters appeared in the *Methodist Recorder*. Some evangelicals lobbied for an evangelical president, and many interpreted this as a protest against the fact that Conference had appointed two presidents in succession who were radical in their views – the previous president had been John Vincent, a leader in the Alliance of Radical Methodists. Donald himself was insistent, in a letter to John Vincent, that the president 'has got to be for all the Methodist people, while having his own particular emphases and beliefs'.[19] Many Methodists felt that at a time when the denomination was wrestling with a number of potentially divisive issues, such as the deliberations on human sexuality, Donald's wisdom, experience and political skills would be of great value. His second presidency was a notable one, with his dominant personality and clear vision standing him in good stead. Yet at the same time he was irenic. He made what he had said before clear in his presidential address: that he did not intend to serve any sectional interest in Methodism. He continued:

> Despite our differences we are one family. Methodists have never expected to agree about everything. There is a fellowship of controversy and, if I may say so, we're pretty good at it! But there is no fellowship of denigration of one another and I hope we will have none of that. We belong together and we need each other. The President is President for all, belonging to no group because belonging to all. Let us make the oneness of our family clear.

Donald took the opportunity in his address to reflect on the twelve-year period since he was last President of Conference. He believed that there was much within Methodist life to celebrate. Programmes like 'Mission Alongside the Poor' and 'Sharing in God's Mission' had, he believed, been fruitful, and had been recognised and used as models by others. He highlighted ethnic issues, welcoming some twenty-six Conference representatives from ethnic minority groups and expressing anticipation of their contribution, as well as

---

[19] D. English to John J. Vincent, 16 August 1989. Also K. Greet to B. Hoare, 13 January 2003. As early as 1972 (11 November) Donald English was the main speaker for the evangelical side at an Evangelical/Radical Consultation. John Vincent was the main speaker for the radical side. The venue was Cliff College. Dialogue continued at a conference in 1973.

that of the increasing numbers of young people at Conference. Donald believed that what was called the 'Ministry of the People of God' – with the first ordinations to the newly reopened Diaconal Order and the beginning of Ministry in Local Appointment – pointed to a much greater experience of the collaborative nature of ministry. Increasing numbers of people were offering for ordination. Almost half of Methodist congregations were recording increases in attendance at worship. Many of Methodism's rural churches were enjoying new life. The 'World Church in Britain' programme was making available the missionary and pastoral insights of Methodists from around the world. Also, the social and political profile of Methodism had, Donald suggested, grown considerably, not least, he emphasised, through the efforts of the last two presidents, Richard Jones and John Vincent.

In typical fashion, Donald then set out challenges facing Methodism. In this address he concentrated on three areas: spirituality, socio-political challenges and evangelism. First, dealing with spirituality, Donald referred to John Wesley's enunciation of 'Scriptural Holiness' or 'perfect love'. Wesley did not believe that Christians would be free from ignorance, mistake, infirmity or temptation, but that the love of God could so control the centre of the believer's being that every thought, attitude, word and deed could issue from divine love. Donald warned against neglecting this core element in Methodist spirituality. He directed attention to prayer and Bible study, fellowship and worship, and the social nature of spirituality, without which he saw holiness as static and even selfish. He also stressed the relationship between spirituality and human personality. Some Christian spiritualities seemed to involve a high level of emotional experience. Others had a strongly cerebral character. Still others were activist. His rather controversial argument was that different spiritualities, together with other 'isms' (as he called them) – radicalism, evangelicalism, sacramentalism, liberalism – answered to different personalities, backgrounds and experiences. 'Christian perfection', Donald proposed, 'holds out the hope that we may all become more fully and roundly developed personalities, and that all of us may learn more tolerance towards the desires and needs of others.'

Secondly, he stressed that it was the Methodist way to be socially and politically involved. In Wesley's terms this was social righteousness. Donald described the Bible as a book about justice. During the Methodist Revival of the eighteenth century, he contended, a whole new class of people was given self-respect. More recently, there had been political encouragement of a new kind, with the demolition of the Berlin Wall. In South Africa there was the beginning of a remarkable transformation. He continued: 'We surely cannot rejoice in the commitment of our sisters and brothers ... and then refuse to be involved in social and political struggles ourselves, unless of course we believe that our society is beyond improvement.' He suggested that the Western 'enterprise culture' was constructed in a way that made casualties inevitable. When Christian ministers spoke about these things, Donald argued, they were not engaging in party politics, but practising pastoral politics. Referring to events in Eastern Europe, he viewed capitalism as showing a ruthless determination to survive, though teetering on the brink of being out of control, whereas the communist or centrally controlled command system was almost everywhere in ruins. Donald asked about a 'third way', a phrase which would be increasingly used by New Labour in the 1990s.

Methodism was also committed, said Donald, to evangelism. He quoted John Wesley's memorable phrase about being called to 'offer them Christ'. In discussing this work, Donald stressed the 'urgent task of apologetics'. This had nothing to do with apologising, but everything to do with defending and advocating the faith where people provided reasons for not believing. For Donald this meant making out the case for a perspective on life often missing from contemporary culture – the presence of the mysterious and the spiritual at the heart of all being. It also meant showing how the good news about Jesus related to events and issues in the daily news. It meant listening to the language and thought-forms of the various academic disciplines, seeking for places where boundaries meet and bridges may be built. Donald argued passionately that a divided Methodism, battling within itself as one group sought precedence over another, would not do this task effectively. He was convinced that the groups within Methodism needed each other for discerning the truth and fulfilling their calling. 'I pray', he concluded, 'that this Connexional Year will see us reaching out to one another in the words which Wesley borrowed from a most unlikely Old Testament text. "Is your heart right, as my heart is with your heart? If it be, please give me your hand." '[20]

By contrast with Donald's concerns when he was involved in setting up CEIM in 1970, there was little attempt in his presidential address of 1990 to emphasise the distinctives that characterised evangelicals. In the 1980s there was an emphasis in Methodism on radicals and evangelicals listening to and learning from each other, and perhaps this process had its effect on evangelical thinking. Evangelicals in Methodism did not want to be seen as those who brought division. Around the time of Donald's second presidency Methodism faced some difficult issues. Donald referred to discussions on human sexuality, and acknowledged that 'we will not agree on all such matters', but rather than offering a perspective on the debates, he commented

---

[20] *Methodist Recorder*, 28 June 1990, pp. 10–11.

that 'we do have a duty to speak out about the moral values which inform our discussion'.[21] It is not clear what this meant. Perhaps it was Donald's ability to listen attentively to different views and to see and state the implications of different points of view that was both his strength and weakness. It was his strength to gain a consensus, but this may have been at times achieved by blurring the sharpness of the disagreements.

At the end of his presidential year, in June 1991, Donald reflected on his experiences at the Ministerial Session of the Conference. He had visited nineteen Districts, together with the Vice-President, Rosemary Wass, and had encountered the diversity of Methodist worship, diversity that he considered much greater than twelve years before. He highlighted four events during the year that he felt were significant. The first two – the establishment of new ecumenical bodies in Britain and the Decade of Evangelism – relate to the chapter in this book on Donald's work in the ecumenical movement. The third was the celebration that had taken place of the 200th anniversary of the death of John Wesley. Donald asked if Methodism was still true to the calling expressed in its Deed of Union, which was 'to spread Scriptural holiness throughout the land by the proclamation of the Evangelical Faith'. His observation, after another year of travelling the Connexion, was:

that many of our best people are almost totally locked up on our premises running the institutional church, while many others avoid being too closely joined to us because they rightly fear that we will do the same to them ... However good the system, if it hinders rather than serves the proclamation of the evangelical faith, then it is less than the best.[22]

---

[21] Ibid, p. 10.
[22] *Methodist Recorder*, 20 June 1991, p. 13.

Donald's final reference was to the big issues in the world that had challenged the Christian church during the year – the Gulf War, the latest developments in genetic engineering and the question of inter-faith relationships. During his year as President Donald addressed these and other issues. He advocated that Christian leaders and those of other faiths, particularly the Muslim community, should formally meet for conversation on the Gulf crisis, to search for whatever common mind might emerge for an approach to government. Leaders in other churches felt this was too difficult. Donald accepted the reluctance and deferred to his ecumenical partners, but he believed that an opportunity had been lost. His own pastoral letters to Methodists always covered world affairs as well as ecclesiastical matters.

It was an abiding passion of Donald's as a Methodist leader that the church should have something relevant to say from the Bible to the world. Here, it can fairly be argued, was the heart of his evangelical faith. Yet it seemed clear that, despite Methodism's concern to be relevant, the denomination was not attracting people as it had done in the past. Some congregations were growing, but from 1960 to 1995 Methodist membership fell from 728,589 to 380,195.[23] Donald's conviction, however, remained that if the gospel were properly applied to people's situations it would have an effect. He stated in 1991 that speaking out about world issues as president had convinced him of 'the importance of our being clear about the nature and relevance of our biblical foundations'. In his meetings with ministers during his presidency he tried to encourage them to understand more deeply the main themes of Scripture – creation, righteousness, redemption – and to show, in their preaching and

---

[23] J.M. Turner, *Modern Methodism in England, 1932–1998* (Peterborough: Epworth Press, 1998), p. 21.

through other means, how these themes were relevant to the issues of the day.[24]

* * * * *

In her own reflections on Donald's leadership, Margaret Parker pointed out that, in spite of the many demands on him in the multiplicity of tasks he undertook, he always had time for individuals. Perhaps it was because of this, she suggests, that he was so effective as a statesman. At meetings he could look out on people he knew personally, people he had encouraged and counselled, including some who had stayed within the ranks of Methodism partly because Donald was there. 'He was', Margaret Parker stated, 'an evangelical statesman who did not flinch from saying what was hard to hear, but who said it with love and compassion; an evangelical statesman who led from the front but gave time to the person struggling at the back.' Methodism responded warmly to leadership of that kind. In the next chapter we look at Donald as a preacher. Here, again, his concern was often for those 'struggling at the back'.

---

[24] *Methodist Recorder*, 20 June 1991, p. 13.

7

Gifted Preacher

For many people, their experience of Donald English was as a preacher. Paul Smith, then Superintendent of the Altrincham Methodist circuit in the north-west of England, wrote in 1999:

> To say that Donald English was a fine Biblical expositor is to state the obvious. As an evangelical Christian he held the Bible in high regard. Like Wesley, he was a man of one book. The clarity of his exposition left his hearers wondering why they had read that passage so often and never grasped its heart before, but it belied the tremendous amount of preparation which such exposition demands. Donald knew that in order to get to the heart of a passage of scripture any preacher must grasp the impact it made on those who first heard its teaching or read its message.[1]

It was during his time with the IVF that Donald became increasingly convinced of the importance of biblical exposition. He often gave testimony to the value to himself of regular personal Bible study, and especially to the early help he had received from the Bible study course published by

---

[1] P. Smith, 'Donald English – Preacher' in Abbott (ed.), *Donald English*, p. 20.

Inter-Varsity Press. This concern to be faithful to the text of Scripture always remained paramount.

But there was more to Donald's preaching than careful exposition, since many preachers have been faithful and dedicated students of the Bible without ever developing and using the medium of preaching in the effective way for which Donald English became so well known. One feature that invariably characterised Donald's preaching was his ability to bring the Bible to life. He had great ability as a storyteller, and saw himself as following the example of Jesus in the Gospels, a Jesus whose stories connected with ordinary people. Donald used his ability to convey the biblical drama and also to earth it in contemporary life. A key element was that he had what W.E. Sangster used to call 'a trawling eye' and was adept at turning incidents and personal experiences – sometimes stories told at his own expense – into extremely telling, clear and often very moving illustrations. He had a natural and apparently effortless gift of speaking in picture language. Apt and memorable phrases lit up his sermons: 'Our believing has become fragmented – more like a bag of marbles than a bunch of grapes!' Those who heard Donald often remembered the vivid word-pictures he painted. Preachers who only dealt in abstract truths were challenged by the way in which Donald brought these truths home by the use of stories set in concrete situations.

It is crucial, in analysing Donald English's preaching, to note his capacity not only to enter imaginatively into the world of Scripture but also to empathise with those he was addressing. It was this, perhaps above everything else, that made his preaching so compelling. Whatever type of group in the church he was speaking to, from children to pensioners, he was somehow able to enter their world. This brought the text of Scripture alive and made it impinge on the hearers' own life experiences in such a way that, even years later, people could recall what Donald had said. Paul Kingston, General Secretary of the Home Mission Department of the Methodist Church in Ireland, who served with Donald in Nigeria in the early 1960s, recalled in the 1990s the first time he heard him speak. Donald preached the Eastern District Synod sermon at the Uzuakoli Leprosy Settlement, reminding his hearers that the Word was to be proclaimed like a town crier would proclaim a message, going through the streets of an African town. The picture stuck in the memory.

Donald's style of preaching developed and changed over the years of his ministry. Laurence Churms, who was best man at Donald and Bertha's wedding, recalls that when they were fellow students Donald was chastised in sermon class for squeezing the life out of his message by over-elaboration. He preached a classic three-point sermon, but had three more points under every main point. As he developed, his style became more varied, and his messages more determinedly shaped by the context of his audience. He was also prepared to invest much personal energy in his preaching. Phillips Brooks spoke of preaching as 'the communication of truth through personality'. It was one of Donald's favourite definitions. Over the period of his ministry his gifts as a communicator were put to good use in addressing groups ranging from a university mission meeting in a smoke-filled student bar to a congregation of High Court judges and barristers at the Judges' Service in the Cathedral Church of St Peter and St Paul Sheffield in 1992. Theologically, this was truly incarnational preaching, which was the result not only of a remarkable set of natural and spiritual gifts but also of a great deal of hard work. Donald's conviction was that if people were to hear and understand the gospel, then the Word must be made flesh: they must see it clothed in their own culture, hear it expressed in their own language and have some sense of commonality with the preacher.

In a message given at a Cliff College conference in 1994, on the theme of 'Preaching: A Lost Art', Donald spoke about the things he had learned during his years as a preacher of the Bible. He had learned firstly, he said, to distinguish between the authority of Scripture and any particular interpretation of Scripture. He had also learned, secondly, to distinguish between eternal truth and any particular local expression of that truth in history. Thirdly, he had learned to distinguish between biblical principles and their varied application to life. All of this emphasises that Donald's concern was to see preachers acting wisely as expositors. In this he was an exemplar for many. Brian Beck, a former Secretary of Conference, writes: 'Donald was an expositor of the Bible. Many of his books illustrate that on the more intimate scale, and on the big stage there was no one better.' Beck continued by noting that, sadly, those invited to give Bible studies in a 'big stage' setting were too often:

> either faithful to the scholarship, above the heads of the audience and dull in consequence, or they appeal to the crowd, soar in eloquence and barely notice the Bible. To listen to Donald doing a Bible study for four thousand people was to hear sound scholarship and fine preaching gifts both used to communicate the Word of God in language people could understand and respond to.

* * * * *

What were those settings in which Donald used his gifts as a preacher to the full? He was, as we have seen, committed to local church ministry. However, he was especially in his element when given the space to expound passages of Scripture in a more extended and systematic way. He rose to the occasion when speaking to large crowds at events such as

the inter-denominational Keswick Convention, the Cliff
College Derwent Week, Easter People, the Baptist Assembly and the World Methodist Council (WMC). In addition
he spoke at many smaller conferences. He was recognised at
these various kinds of events as both an incisive contributor
and an effective populariser, although his was never a
superficial kind of popularising, and he was able to bring
the fruits of fine biblical scholarship within the grasp of
ordinary people. As we will see, his studies delivered to
audiences of thousands from all over the world at the WMC
conferences in Dublin and Nairobi won him standing
ovations as well as invitations to travel to different parts of
the world as a visiting preacher. It was his commitment to
biblical study and exposition – which he always saw as
foundational to any sermon or address, whether a sixty-
minute Bible study or a three-minute devotional opening to
a committee meeting – that meant he was invited for the
first time to the Keswick Convention in 1974.

Relatively few Methodists have been prominent at
Keswick. Charles Inwood, an Irish Methodist minister, was
very well known to early twentieth-century Keswick audiences. A Methodist lay person, Fred Mitchell, was an
influential Keswick figure and Chair of the Convention in the
late 1940s, and Arthur Skevington Wood, at one time Principal of Cliff College, was also a Keswick speaker. In the earlier
period of the Convention's life, from its inception in 1875,
there was disagreement between some within the (largely
Anglican) leadership of Keswick over the doctrine of sanctification. Wesleyan holiness spirituality was regarded with
some suspicion at Keswick.[2] A century later such disputes
were no longer regarded as relevant; none the less, Keswick
speakers still tended on the whole to be Anglican, Baptist or
Presbyterian, not Methodist. Donald English gave the Bible

[2] C. Price and I. Randall, *Transforming Keswick* (Carlisle:
Paternoster, 2000), ch. 3.

readings – a series of Bible expositions during the Keswick Convention week – on four occasions, in 1980, 1984, 1988 and 1993. In August 1993, after he had given the Bible readings on Paul's letter to the Galatians (under the frequently used theme at Keswick, 'The Life of Faith'), Donald wrote to the Chair of Keswick, Philip Hacking, to ask for feedback on his ministry. This is a sign of Donald's desire always to be relevant. He particularly asked whether there had been any complaints about his stress on the implications of faith for life in the world. At one point Donald had said this:

> I was in Lancashire, down below a great big [Methodist] Central Hall where I was conducting worship up above; but below the dregs of the city, to be frank, were gathering. And sitting in the midst of all that was a huge man in a rather old pullover, loving them for Jesus' sake ... I felt, why am I going upstairs to lead worship? Where would Jesus be? I think he would have sent a substitute upstairs and stayed below.[3]

Philip Hacking replied to Donald's letter to say that the Bible readings Donald had given had been received positively, and he also suggested that ten years before they might have received a less positive response from the Keswick audience. Keswick's inclination had been to address personal holiness rather than world-related ministry. Donald commented in September 1993: 'My own experience of Keswick, and of evangelical conventions elsewhere, is that if one can show that one's conclusions are based on scripture, or at least are possible interpretations of the meaning of scripture for today, then people are willing to receive and listen and ponder.'[4]

---

[3] D. English, 'Coming and Going', Mark 3:13–19, Keswick Convention, 1993.

[4] D. English to P. Hacking, 27 August 1993; P. Hacking to D. English, 31 August 1993; D. English to P. Hacking, 6 September 1993.

The confidence Donald had about preaching was not, however, confined to preaching at specifically evangelical events. During the 1980s and 1990s Donald was a sought-after preacher and speaker at many special occasions. In 1979 he delivered a sermon in Westminster Abbey for the 150th anniversary of the Metropolitan Police. The number of such occasions multiplied. They included an address to the Royal College of Veterinary Surgeons in 1983; an address on Christian discipleship and public leadership given in the House of Lords in 1988; an address on 'John Wesley: Reverend, Revivalist or Revolutionary?' as Leicester University 'Graduate of the Year', also in 1988; and a sermon in St Paul's Cathedral on 24 May 1988 – Wesley Day. In the 1990s his special addresses included one given to the Lawyers' Christian Fellowship at the Temple Church; a talk on 'Christianity and Politics' delivered at the Department of Politics of Queen's University, Belfast; sermons for Oxford, Cambridge and London universities; an address at a special service in 1996 commemorating the founding of the United Nations; and an address to a consultation on wealth creation at St George's House, Windsor. When he spoke at these events Donald was always well informed, although he never tried to claim knowledge that he did not possess. A typical letter of appreciation was the one from the Metropolitan Commissioner of Police, Sir David McNee, who said that the relevance of Donald's sermon had been commented upon widely. People appreciated Donald's informed references to the police, both past and present.[5]

Donald English loved opportunities to communicate outside the normal church settings, and rose to the challenge of tuning into the different wavelengths on which people operated in their thinking. Paul Smith has this to say about Donald's addresses:

[5] D. McNee to D. English, 4 June 1979.

He had the ability to identify trends, analyse forces and grasp issues. Convinced as he was that there is no situation in which the gospel has nothing to say, he would bring his understanding of the biblical message to bear on his understanding of society and personal need in a way which convinced his hearers that he really understood them, their needs and the difference which the gospel could make. Maybe that is why he endeared himself to so many. He knew what made people tick.[6]

It was partly this gift of understanding people that made Donald's preaching so full of interest and enabled him to hold people's attention. On occasions – but only when it was appropriate – he would speak for considerably longer periods of time than the normal twenty minutes that marks the stopping point for most preachers. Some have thought him rather self-indulgent on that score. He would not have claimed to be any more immune to that temptation than any other preacher. However, the nature and length of his addresses was due to the requirements of his subject rather than to any desire for self-promotion.

An example of Donald's effectiveness outside the ordinary church context is provided by one Methodist minister, J. Keith Jackson. In 1974, at which time he was a local preacher, Jackson and his family moved to Bristol, since Jackson was taking up the post of Director of Resource Planning with Wessex Water Authority. The family joined the Westbury-on-Trym Methodist Church where Donald, Bertha and their two sons worshipped. Jackson writes:

My first encounter with Donald the preacher–teacher was when he spoke to our Wesley Guild and I was astounded at the brilliant manner in which he brought his bible study alive for us. Then in due course I heard him preach many times and was

---

[6] Smith, 'Donald English – Preacher' in Abbott (ed.), *Donald English*, p. 21.

always struck by his thought provoking evangelical sermons invariably delivered in a most appealing manner.

About the time of Donald's first term as President of Conference, Jackson's chief at Wessex Water Authority asked him to come up with suggestions for a guest speaker for the organisation's dining club. Speakers had included an ombudsman, a Concorde design engineer and an authority on Isambard Kingdom Brunel. Later, Jackson said, 'Do you think it would be OK if I could manage to persuade our current President of the Methodist Conference to come and speak to us?'

This was agreed and arranged, and when Donald started his address he immediately connected with his audience. He said: 'From what I have heard, I believe you are an organisation with a keen interest in training, and so tonight I hope to share with you some of my own insights as a trainer of personnel for full-time service in the Methodist Ministry.' A colleague of Jackson's, in giving a hearty vote of thanks to Donald, said: 'I think we must agree, gentlemen, that having received lots of advice from all sorts of management consultants, here at last we the Wessex team have been brought face to face with something really worthwhile.' As a result of Donald's powerful Christian witness that evening he was subsequently invited to address the south-west branch of the Institution of Civil Engineers in Bath. Jackson himself later became an ordained minister.

These examples of the way in which Donald could engage with business and civic leaders could be multiplied many times. He eagerly utilised such opportunities, not necessarily for direct evangelism, but often for apologetic purposes. He often referred to apologetics as 'making space' for evangelism.

On many occasions Donald was invited to be the mission-er at directly evangelistic events. A few of these missions were

on a large scale. David Mullins, a Methodist minister
in York, was instrumental with John Young and others in
bringing into being an ecumenical mission in York
in 1992, which was entitled 'One Voice', and at which
Donald was the main speaker. Over 300 churches in York
and the surrounding area participated. Mullins describes
how Donald was greatly in favour of using a neutral venue
and encouraged the planning group for 'One Voice' to
look at the possibility of using the soon-to-be-opened
Barbican Centre. Donald wanted people to engage with
the gospel on their own territory, where they felt comfortable, even though walking out on to an empty stage to
preach was not familiar to him. Donald said at one
planning meeting that he wanted all those who came to
the mission to have 'a good entertaining experience'. That
remark, Mullins suggests, set the direction for the mission:
evangelism through entertainment. Evenings at the Barbican featured the York Bach Choir, the Riding Lights
Theatre Company, Geoffrey Stevenson the mime artist,
and other musicians and actors. The address by Donald
was part of this wider programme. One woman, who had
no prior faith commitment, made a comment to a local
minister that it was 'entertainment with a message', and
another couple spoke about 'entertainment that makes
you think'.

But the message was still central and crucial. Donald
made it clear to those involved in the mission that for him
the gospel message included seven vital elements:

1. The message had to be biblical and in keeping with
   God's revelation of himself in Scripture. It had to be
   Christological.
2. The aim was to make disciples, not merely converts. The
   cost of discipleship had to be included: the dying to self
   and rising with Christ.

3. There had to be an apologetic element so that the reasons people had for not believing were listened to and answered.
4. It had to be related to daily life and people had to see that it affected the way they lived.
5. There had to be teaching content for the mind as well as an appeal to the heart.
6. The social implications of the gospel had to be explored, so that it was clear that Christ was involved in the whole of life.
7. It had to be ecumenical. Donald said that it undercut the gospel of reconciliation when Christians could not get together to tell it.

The central element of each evening was the address given by Donald. These addresses had been scheduled at thirty minutes, but they often overran, sometimes by as much as ten minutes, although Donald completely held his audience. His talks were based on stories that Jesus told, or incidents in his life, and were given contemporary titles that stimulated interest:

WHY BOTHER?	Luke 10:25–37	Good Samaritan
JUST ONE MORE THING	Mark 10:17–27	Rich Young Ruler
LAST HEARD OF …	Luke 15:11–24	Prodigal Son
ALL EXPENSES PAID	Matthew 20:1–16	Labourers in the Vineyard
COMING CLEAN	Mark 5:21–43	Woman with a haemorrhage
BUT IS IT TRUE?	John 20:19–29	Doubting Thomas
JOB DESCRIPTION AVAILABLE	Luke 14:25–35	Becoming a Disciple

Donald prepared meticulously for these evangelistic addresses. The scripts for the seven addresses show that each
one was carefully crafted. Each message was based on a
biblical passage, but in addition to the attention to the texts,
what Donald said was packed full of captivating references
to everyday life. As always, Donald spoke with sparkling
humour. Because he was in York, he often used illustrations
from his time in the RAF on national service at nearby
Linton-on-Ouse. He seemed very much at home on the
stage. He stood centre stage with a small table to his right;
on it was a glass of water and a small Bible, to which he
referred occasionally. Donald established an excellent
rapport with his audience and made the story of Jesus come
alive in a very real way. Donald was not afraid of emotion
and on a few occasions was clearly profoundly moved himself as he spoke. This was particularly so as he came to the
subject of the cross and the death of Jesus, which featured in
each of his addresses.

The York mission is also a good example of the way in
which Donald's biblical exposition and graphic storytelling
were combined with a high degree of personal animation. It
was during his 1990 presidency that he decided to take the
bold step of speaking from in front of the pulpit rather than
from behind it. It was a significant and characteristic move,
one which was to manifest itself in the evangelistic setting
during the 'One Voice' mission, when he did not use a
lectern at all, so that there was nothing to impede direct
communication with his hearers. Donald's consuming
desire was to communicate truth to his hearers in a way that
not only informed their minds, but moved their hearts and
wills, and he was concerned to try to remove as many barriers to that process as possible. He was also aware of the
place of his own personality. As a preacher, whether in
evangelistic settings or elsewhere, once the adrenaline
began to flow, his whole body came alive, and his hands,

which were seldom still, would almost 'speak'. When he was not behind a pulpit it could be observed that the same was true of his feet!

During 'One Voice', and on other occasions, Donald was insistent that after the good news had been preached there should be opportunity for those who had heard it to make their own response. Indeed, a response was demanded. David King, Superintendent of Plymouth Central Hall, noted that it had been said of Donald that 'when he preached to thousands you thought he was just talking to you'. Donald was interested in individuals. It was his ability to speak directly to the situations that people faced which contributed to the response that there was to his appeals. Those who were not committed to Christ or to service within the church felt that they had to make a choice. For his part, Donald was eager to encourage a public affirmation of that decision. After he had preached, and as the closing hymn of a meeting was being sung, he would invite people who wished to do so to come forward to the communion rail, when the meeting was being held in a church building. At the communion rail Donald would encourage people to kneel and pray. When it was appropriate, Donald would find out the names of those that had come forward and had made a significant decision. He did not feel that he needed to be involved as a counsellor at the time – although that did happen – but he did want to pray afterwards for people who had made a commitment.

Donald was one of a comparatively few Methodist preachers in the post-war decades who used the 'altar call' after preaching, but it had been his practice from early on in his ministry. The 'altar call' was not unknown in British Methodism, and indeed had been picked up from Methodism by, for example, the Salvation Army. Donald not only incorporated it in his practice but also encouraged other Methodists to do the same. Joe Hale recalls how in the late

1970s Donald preached in Waynesville, North Carolina, USA, one Sunday morning to a congregation of approaching 500 people, and did what was then an unheard of thing in those particular Methodist circles and gave an invitation to people to respond. Many people did so. In later years Donald elaborated his thinking on this matter in a pamphlet entitled *Renewing the Altar Call*, published by the Home Mission Division.

The procedure adopted at 'One Voice', as outlined by David Mullins, was that Donald spent perhaps five or more minutes after each talk outlining ways in which people might respond to the message that night. This could mean, for example, a greater commitment to the poor, a new commitment to Christ, a first step in exploring what being a Christian might mean, a new openness to other Christians from other traditions, or involvement in a new area of Christian service. Initially the response was limited, but Donald said that he believed he should continue to invite people to come forward, and that he should accept responsibility as the evangelist to make the invitation. On the third evening of the mission, after Donald had spoken on the Prodigal Son, he issued the invitation to respond and a much larger number came forward. All those who came were joined by 'listeners' who later talked with them. From that evening onwards the numbers responding each evening grew until the stage was full of people on the last evening. This response was a significant indicator of the power of Donald's evangelistic preaching.

Donald English also took the leading role as preacher at a highly significant mission in Plymouth in 1997. This was his last major mission. He had undertaken a mission in Plymouth in 1976 entitled 'Power for Life' and was a regular visitor there. The 1997 mission, 'Making Waves', was based on the York mission. David King describes how he, together with Prebendary John Watson, then Vicar at St

Andrew's Parish Church in the centre of Plymouth, Ian Coffey, the Minister of Mutley Baptist Church, and Barry Killick, then Pastor of the Plymouth Christian Centre (Pentecostal), went to visit Donald at his office at Central Hall, Westminster. As a result of the conversation, Donald said he would pray and think seriously about the possibility of an ecumenical mission, and he eventually agreed to be the main speaker. The mission made a great impact. It was held in the Plymouth Pavilions, one of the south-west's largest venues, and thousands flocked there for the eight nights of the mission. No other event has attracted so many people for so many consecutive nights to this huge venue. The whole experience brought the churches into the public eye and in many cases gave participating churches fresh confidence in mission. There were stories of conversions and baptisms and of churches taking new initiatives. Most of the 173 people who responded during the mission were from within the churches, but the effects went further.[7] One church started a holiday club resulting from the children's work linked with 'Making Waves'.

Reflecting on 'Power for Life', John Watson of St Andrew's Parish Church, who worked closely with Donald in the Plymouth missions in 1976 and 1997, saw it as of major significance. He highlighted especially the evangelistic talks Donald gave in St Andrew's at lunchtime. Watson described Donald as a man with 'his head in the heavens and his feet on the ground, and with a real grip on the human situation'. He tells of the crowd of business people who attended, starting with approximately 200 people on the Monday, and growing to about 600 people by the end of the week. Kevin Tunstall, another participant, wrote to Donald after 'Making Waves': 'Your talks were innovative, challenging and right on the button.' People had listened

---

[7] J. Howden, 'Making Waves Report', July 1996.

carefully to Donald's addresses, delivered without notes. In Tunstall's view the churches in Plymouth had never seemed to make headway, but he believed this had changed.[8] As an evangelistic preacher Donald had the confidence of many leaders from different denominations. This was part of the role he played as 'more than a Methodist'.

Donald's gifts as an evangelistic communicator were used in many other ways. He spoke, for example, at local missions in Blackpool (1983), Epsom (1987), Bath (1990) and Cork (1995). From the 1980s he was often heard on 'Thought for the Day', and these talks involved him in carefully crafting relevant messages. He also spoke on a number of local radio stations, such as BBC Radio Stoke and Radio Kent. On one occasion he gave a series of talks on the BBC World Service. Donald was fully aware that the method used in preaching was not suitable to the medium of radio. His radio scripts show that he timed his material to the second, even counting the number of words. This thoroughness was an important element in making him an acclaimed communicator on radio. John Barrett recalls that during the Gulf War the BBC was keen to have a balanced Christian reflection on the conflict. The BBC asked Donald, who was at that time President of Conference, to preach on the subject on the Radio 4 Sunday morning service. Although Donald was by this time an experienced studio radio broadcaster, he said that he wanted to preach to a real congregation about the subject, rather than give a studio address. At short notice Barrett arranged for the morning service at his own Methodist Church to move to 9.30am and it was broadcast live on 3 February 1991.

Increasingly Donald was asked to lecture on topics connected with preaching and communication. Methodists and others sought to learn from someone whose own

---

[8] K. Tunstall to D. English, 18 March 1996.

preaching was so effective. In 1983, for example, he gave the annual Laing Lecture at London Bible College. In this lecture he urged that effective communication in mission must 'begin where people are: be concerned with what they now know and do; and speak in language which they understand'. For Donald the ministry of Jesus was the supreme example of this kind of communication.[9] Donald was always keen to address lay preachers. He often referred to his own memories of the Methodist local preachers in the north-east of England where he grew up and the impression that they had made on him as people rooted in their communities and determined to expound the Scriptures properly. In turn Donald encouraged and advised Methodist lay preachers in gatherings at Cliff College and was also invited to speak to Baptist lay preachers. He spoke at the national Evangelists' Conference, organised annually by the Evangelical Alliance, at The Hayes conference centre, Swanwick, in 1991.

In 1992 Donald gave the first of the Beeson lectures at the well-known Asbury Theological Seminary in Kentucky, USA. His subject (indeed, the subject of the lectureship) was preaching. Always a realist, Donald stressed that preaching was facing an enormous challenge. Television had seen to it that the preacher was no longer the best entertainment in town and many who still came faithfully to church none the less found it difficult to be committed to preaching of any kind. Against this background, Donald affirmed his belief in and commitment to biblical preaching. 'By biblical preaching', he explained, 'I do not mean simply the use of a text or the exposition of a passage. I mean that the preacher feels herself, feels himself, to be under the authority of Scripture.' In line with his consistent convictions, however,

---

[9] D. English ' "Tell it as it is": Some Reflections on Communicating the Gospel Today', *Vox Evangelica* XIV (1994), p. 12.

he went on to argue that the preacher needed to know the context in which people lived. Having established the importance of the text and the contemporary context, he then outlined the themes he believed were important in preaching, the first of these being God's transcendence and immanence. Biblical preaching, he argued, would demonstrate the relative nature of everything in life except the claim of God, who is transcendent and in the midst. Donald's conviction was that preaching should subject all human values to the severe judgement of God. At the same time, biblical preaching would affirm that everything in the spiritual life depends on God's initiative in Christ and on the human response to Christ. The secret of power, he maintained, was the secret found in Jesus. Real power rested not with a God who was only transcendent but with the suffering, serving, dying and rising Jesus.

The book that emerged as a result of these lectures, *An Evangelical Theology of Preaching*, represents probably Donald's greatest achievement as a writer. What is striking about his reflections on preaching is that they are shot through with theology. This is not a 'how-to' manual for preachers. The book deals with creation and redemption. Donald outlined the Catholic approach, which affirms continuity between nature and grace, and the Protestant approach, which has often spoken about discontinuity and about a world infected by sinfulness. Donald underlined the challenge of the gospel as a call to a new and changed life. He also argued, however, that there was a danger the Christian could be cut off from the world, and he commended a strong doctrine of creation. Preachers should speak of God at work outside the church.[10] In his chapter on the atonement, repentance and conversion he suggested that as well

---

[10] D. English, *An Evangelical Theology of Preaching* (Nashville: Abingdon Press, 1996), ch. 2.

as preaching the traditional theories of the atonement there could be great benefit in preachers looking at the atonement in new ways. The two he proposed were, firstly, the cross as God's entry into and bearing of human suffering and, secondly, the cross as a model for self-giving to the poor.[11] Other chapters dealt with such topics as reason and faith, the gospel and life, evangelistic preaching, being interesting, and what kind of person the preacher should be. In his introduction Donald recalled Methodist local preachers who served as examples. 'Preaching was not so much what they did as what they were.'[12]

*   *   *   *   *

In a fine tribute to Donald English, Brian Beck, who as Secretary of Conference had a wide-ranging perspective, described Donald as first of all an evangelist. Beck elaborated in this way:

> He gave his life to Jesus Christ as a young man and longed for others to do the same. He was an evangelical in the technical sense; holding firmly to the authority of the Bible as the Word of God, making all his judgements in the light of that, and never losing that devotion to Scripture or that desire for others to be converted to Jesus Christ.

Wherever Donald was – in a Sunday service, at a Cliff College weekend, at an ecumenical mission at which he was guest preacher, on 'Thought for the Day' on Radio 4 – it was this commitment, Beck suggests, that drove him on, 'and into it, whether in preparation or in delivery, he put all his energy'. For Donald there was no greater calling than to

---

[11] Ibid. ch. 4.
[12] Ibid. p. 12.

be a preacher of the good news of Jesus Christ. He looked for responses to the message from the people to whom he spoke and he also hoped to inspire other preachers to excitement about the message and the many ways in which it could be proclaimed. This desire for effective communication of the gospel was something for which Donald was known not only within Methodism but also in ecumenical circles.

8

Ecumenical Enthusiast

From his earliest period as an active Christian, Donald
English was ecumenical in his interests. This was expressed, as we have seen, in his involvement in the inter-
denominational Inter-Varsity Fellowship (IVF). His wide
sympathies were also evident during his time in Nigeria.
Towards the end of his time as minister at Cullercoats, in
1971, he was invited to be one of the ten Methodists who,
together with ten Anglicans, would make up the Standing
Anglican–Methodist Liaison Committee which the two
churches had decided to set up.[1] There were hopes at that
time for Anglican–Methodist union. Even when this did
not materialise, the committee continued to meet and to
consider theological issues. Donald assumed a much more
prominent place within the ecumenical scene in Britain
when he was appointed Chair of the National Initiative for
Evangelism (NIE). He served in this role from 1978 until
1983, when the NIE was disbanded. His ecumenical involvement continued through the pan-denominational
missions he undertook. In 1986 to 1987 he was Moderator
of the Free Church Federal Council. Finally, under the new
ecumenical bodies that were set up to replace the British
Council of Churches (BCC), Donald was Chair of the

---

[1] K. Greet, Secretary of the Conference, to Donald English, 14
September 1971.

Churches Together in England Co-ordinating Group for Evangelisation.

Although the immediate hopes that many had for Anglican–Methodist union were dashed in 1972, when the Church of England did not approve the scheme by a sufficient majority, those who were keen to pursue ecumenical possibilities continued, in spite of their disappointment, to engage in discussions. In 1964, at Nottingham, 550 delegates from 15 denominations had passed a resolution inviting BCC member churches to work for unity in 1980, and it was regarded as significant that for the first time evangelicals were represented in some strength at such a conference.[2] Talks about unity were, therefore, continuing in the 1970s, and these talks included representatives from the Roman Catholic and Orthodox churches as well as Protestant denominations. Donald English was present at a two-day conference at Mansfield College, Oxford, in December 1973 as a Methodist representative. On this occasion there were representatives from the Baptist Union (eight), the Churches of Christ (one), the Church of England (seven), the Free Church Federal Council (three), the Lutheran Council of Great Britain (two), the Methodist Church (six), the Greek Orthodox Church (two), the Roman Catholic Church (eight) and the United Reformed Church (eight). The United Reformed Church (URC) had been formed in 1972 by the union of the English and Welsh Congregationalists and the English Presbyterians. There was considerable discussion at this conference of a scheme for ecumenical progress put forward by Donald English.[3]

The handwritten notes of Donald's talk on that occasion show that he stressed the dangers of a 'ready-made' scheme for unity. He argued for an approach that looked at schemes

---

[2] *The Christian*, 25 September 1964, p. 1.
[3] Notes of a meeting, 'Talks about Talks', 10–11 December 1973, at Mansfield College, Oxford.

already underway in Areas of Ecumenical Experiment (AEE) to see by what processes union had become a reality. This could, he proposed, be done by a special commission. He also called for more theological reflection on the issues that were raised by these local schemes. He proposed three years of study and work towards a new model of unity. Referring to the Anglican–Methodist scheme, Donald suggested that one lesson to be learned from the failure of that scheme was that there was a misguided sense of urgency. Local feelings had not been sufficiently consulted. Donald had been very concerned in the period before the Anglican–Methodist scheme failed that nearly a quarter of Conference had voted against it.[4] Leading Methodists had recognised, however, that it was likely to be the Anglicans who could not achieve a 75 per cent majority in favour of the scheme in Synod,[5] and this is what proved to be the case. Against this background, Donald proposed that in ecumenical talks there should be 'appropriate urgency, but careful urgency'.[6] Almost all of those who responded to Donald's paper agreed that his ideas were worth pursuing and he was asked to present them in fuller form.

This was done at a meeting at Westminster Central Hall on 5 February 1974. Again, about forty-five people were present, most of whom had been at the Oxford meeting. Donald English's paper was a major item for discussion and he reiterated a number of the points he had made in Oxford two months earlier. This time, however, he dealt with wider theological and ecclesial issues. He argued that the 1964 Nottingham Covenant, although courageous, did not command denominational commitment. He applauded the formation of the URC, but emphasised the Anglican–

---

[4] D. English to K. Greet, 10 November 1971.

[5] K. Greet to D. English, 12 November 1971.

[6] Handwritten notes, typed up after the meeting at Mansfield College.

Methodist failure. He also criticised the book *Growing into Union*, authored in 1970 by two well-known evangelicals, J.I. Packer and Colin Buchanan, and two leading Anglo-Catholics, Graham Leonard and Eric Mascall. This book, espousing evangelical–Anglo-Catholic co-operation, had caused some tensions within British evangelicalism.[7] Donald felt that *Growing into Union* did not take enough account of the connexional nature of a denomination like Methodism and he insisted that, as he saw it, any new ecumenical schemes must take the experience of local churches seriously as well as recognising the importance of the church universal. He was strongly of the opinion that an ecumenical commission should be set up, which would engage in wide-ranging investigation.[8]

In response to Donald's paper, fellow Methodist and Secretary of Conference Kenneth Greet said that any way forward must depend on the goodwill of the lower levels of the church. John Huxtable, however, General Secretary of United Reformed Church, said that people in local ecumenical projects looked to national leaders for guidance. David Russell, General Secretary of the Baptist Union, considered that the right aim was 'agreement in faith, order and mission'. The Bishop of St Edmundsbury and Ipswich, L.W. Brown, although noting that the Church of England was 'not yet ready to negotiate', welcomed Donald English's approach and suggested a declaration of intent as a basis on which to build. A Roman Catholic participant, on the other hand, R.L. Stewart, commented that AEEs as they currently

---

[7] C.O. Buchanan, E.L. Mascall, J.I. Packer and Graham Leonard, *Growing into Union: Proposals for Forming a United Church* (London: SPCK, 1970); see I.M. Randall and D. Hilborn, *One Body in Christ: The History and Significance of the Evangelical Alliance* (Carlisle: Paternoster Press, 2001), pp. 253–6.

[8] D. English, 'Church Union Talks: A Possible Way Forward', unpublished paper, 14 January 1974.

stood provided little in the way of models for Roman Catholics. Only three out of forty had Roman Catholic involvement. After hearing these and other comments Donald said that he was prepared to rewrite the section of his paper on AEEs, but he believed that local ecumenical co-operation was a sign of what could be achieved in the future.[9] Over the next three decades it would become clear that Donald was right. Little was to be achieved in the way of structural ecumenism at national level, whereas local ecumenism steadily advanced.

Donald was delighted in the mid-1970s by the increasing interest in evangelism that seemed to be evident across the denominations and he saw evangelistic activity as the most constructive way in which different churches could work together. Three streams seemed to be flowing together in the period 1974 to 1976. The first was the 'Call to the Nation' by the Archbishops Donald Coggan of Canterbury and Stuart Blanch of York in 1975. The second was an attempt to bring Billy Graham to the UK again. Those involved were the Billy Graham Evangelistic Association, the Evangelical Alliance and the Church of England Evangelical Council. An Evangelicals' Working Party produced a programme and plan for church growth, entitled *Let My People Grow*. The third stream came from the ecumenical movement. The World Council of Churches (WCC) Assembly at Nairobi in 1976 produced a sense of convergence among evangelicals, Roman Catholics and those in the WCC over evangelism. In April 1976 the Methodist Church brought a proposal to the BCC that perhaps the Archbishop of Canterbury should convene a meeting of all those interested in finding a way forward in evangelism on a national scale. A group met in October 1976 and six months later a proposal was put to the major churches and Christian

---

[9] Minutes of a meeting at Westminster Central Hall, 4–5 February 1974.

organisations that there should be a nationwide initiative in evangelism. At the end of 1977 the NIE, as it was always called, was born.

The first meeting of the Initiative Committee, with Donald as Chair, was held in March 1978. Donald wrote in June 1978: 'We believe very deeply that God is doing a new thing in calling together so widely representative a group of His people to work together. We are not clear yet as to the exact shape the work or the resulting evangelism will take.'[10] The committee's aim was initially defined as being to stimulate and encourage intelligent proclamation of the gospel. Later the word 'evangelism' was substituted for the phrase 'proclamation of the gospel'. At its second meeting the Initiative Committee agreed that it would spend at least an hour of each meeting in prayer, in addition to the chair's opening devotions. Donald usually gave a Bible study within these devotions, and Sylvia Mary Alison, an Anglican lay person, often shared her visions for NIE, which were usually in the form of pictures. Donald said that 'we remembered them clearly and could refer back to them months later when all the other talking had long since been forgotten'.[11]

On 22 January 1979 the dedication service of the NIE was held. The launch was, significantly, during the Week of Prayer for Christian Unity and was within a service in Lambeth Palace Chapel at which 120 people were present. These included the Archbishop of Canterbury, Cardinal Archbishop of Westminster, the President of the Methodist Conference, the Moderator of the Free Church Federal Council, the Primus of Scotland, the President of the Evangelical Alliance, the British Commissioner of the Salvation Army and other leaders. Donald gave the address and spoke

[10] R. Whitehead and A. Sneddon, *An Unwanted Child?: The story of NIE* (London: BCC/CCBI, 1990), p. 12.

[11] Ibid. p.13; S.M. Alison, *God is Building a House* (Alresford: John Hunt, 2002), pp. 48–52, 96–7.

of the historic nature of the occasion. 'Many of us', he said, 'have previously worshipped with some others who are here, but never before have we all worshipped together in this way.' He believed that at national level such a service had never taken place in England before. There was an acknowledgement that those present represented different degrees of commitment to the Initiative – and this would become more apparent later – but all were present to commend the Initiative. Donald noted that on a day marked by strikes in Britain – themselves, as he said, symbols of unreconciliation and distrust – what had happened in Lambeth Palace Chapel was that 'the leaders of most of the Christians in England took a decisive step towards reconciliation and stronger trust within the body of Christ'.[12]

By February 1979 about 250 letters of support for and enquiry about the Initiative had been received. In the autumn of 1979 Donald began to hold meetings with church leaders. As part of this round of meetings, he was the first non-Anglican to address the Anglican House of Bishops. He worked with the Executive Secretary of NIE, David Taylor, who was an Anglican lay reader. It was decided to have a NIE Assembly in 1980. The key idea, which it was hoped would be expressed in the assembly, was of convergence in mission. Donald realised that there were problems with this concept. People in different streams of the church might be converging, but did they still have different ideas about the gospel? He felt, however, that the idea was well worth pursuing and that the NIE provided 'the possibility of an evangelistic shape to ecumenical relationships'.[13] He hoped that NIE encouragement would stimulate local evangelism – in local churches and in regions. NIE co-ordinated a 'Call to Prayer' for the first Sunday in 1980. It was based on the

---

[12] An Address given at the Dedication Service of the NIE by the Reverend Donald English, NIE Papers.

[13] Whitehead and Sneddon, *An Unwanted Child?*, p. 24.

Methodist Covenant Service, which takes place on that
Sunday each year. One hundred thousand covenant cards
were distributed. The NIE committee estimated that 5,000
to 6,000 churches had participated. The press coverage
was, however, very limited, and there was some pressure
for NIE to abandon its quieter approach and adopt a cam-
paigning strategy. In its answer to the question whether the
NIE should be more activist or more reflective, the NIE
Council of Reference, which had representatives from the
major denominations, was deeply divided. Donald English,
seeking to find the middle ground, said: 'Our very existence
is a sign.'[14] The dilemma was not resolved.

Another dilemma was the NIE's relationship with the
Evangelical Alliance (EA). Donald visited the Evangelical
Alliance Council in order to build relationships with that
constituency. He was himself a member of the EA. At a residential conference of the EA on 30 and 31 January 1978
involvement in NIE was discussed. Gordon Landreth, the
EA General Secretary, reported that Evangelicals had been
asked to play a major role in choosing the Initiative Committee.[15] At a meeting of the Executive Council of the EA in
September 1978 it was agreed that Clifford Hill, the EA's
Secretary for Evangelism and Church Growth, would work
as closely as possible with the NIE Secretary. Donald English
said that he considered that NIE and EA ideas were virtually
identical and hoped that there would be agreed spheres of
co-operation.[16] In 1979 a formula was worked out with the
EA by which the EA and NIE would work at different levels
and in different areas. The EA had a year of evangelism in
1980 led by Clifford Hill and in the same year Donald spoke

---

[14] Ibid. p. 30.

[15] Minutes of the Residential Session of the Executive Council of
the Evangelical Alliance held on 30–31 January 1978.

[16] Minutes of a Special Meeting of the Executive Council of the
Evangelical Alliance, 12 September 1978.

at an EA Congress at Prestatyn, Wales. The 2,000 people present were part of an EA Assembly, a ministers' gathering and Spring Harvest. Donald said it was the most open, questioning EA gathering he had attended.[17] There was discussion in this period about an invitation to Billy Graham to return to the UK. However, the Council of Reference of the NIE would not support this. Donald met with Billy Graham and for a time the response of the NIE to his visit became the test, in some people's eyes, of the NIE's thinking about evangelism. In the event Graham decided not to come.

Gordon Landreth, who was a member of the Initiative Committee and the NIE Council of Reference, wrote:

I saw Donald at work both chairing the NIE Committee and also as a member of its Council of Reference. I was acutely aware of his considerable skills in holding together a very disparate group from different church traditions and drawing out the good in all of them. He was such a gracious man and much loved by all in the Initiative. There was no doubt of his skills as a chairman. I also remember vividly what a brilliant Bible expositor Donald was, both in meetings connected with the NIE and in other conferences in which I was also involved in the '70s. He would open up a passage quietly, logically, and so persuasively, and it was easy to recall his points and the thrust of the message.

Landreth continued:

Donald undoubtedly was a hard worker, and took on many commitments, but he never seemed flustered and had time for people ... As I drew towards the end of my time as General Secretary of the Evangelical Alliance Donald tried to persuade me to take up a position in the British Council of Churches, believ-

---

[17] Whitehead and Sneddon, *An Unwanted Child?*, p. 32.

ing that I would have a significant contribution to make in such a role. I confess that (unlike Donald) I was feeling rather worn out by the tensions of ecumenical relations by that time, and did not think it right to consider his proposal further. Donald himself clearly had much to give in those circles for some years to come. Donald and I had a warm friendship in those work situations and I felt he was a person with whom I could share my deeper feelings and problems.

The NIE event that had the highest profile was a National Assembly, held from 22 to 27 September 1980 in Nottingham. There were 822 full-time participants, with over 950 at the plenary sessions. Of these, 51 per cent were Anglicans, 12 per cent were Methodists, 11 per cent were Baptists, 10 per cent were URC, 4 per cent were Catholics and 12 per cent were 'others', including Brethren, Pentecostal, Independent and black-majority churches. It was a widely representative gathering. There were well-known speakers such as Robert Runcie, Archbishop of Canterbury, John A. Newton, the President-Designate of the Methodist Conference, Stuart Blanch, the Archbishop of York, Henry Wansbrough of Ampleforth College (later Master of St Benet's Hall, University of Oxford), the evangelical Anglican leader John Stott and Roy Clements, minister of Eden Baptist Chapel, Cambridge. The opening and closing sessions of the conference owed, it was widely recognised, a considerable debt to Donald's excellent chairmanship. In the closing address to the conference, Donald stressed convergence. He said:

> From the time I first really began to understand what it meant to be a Christian, I was raised as an evangelical. And I don't apologise for that at all. I thank God for it. But I have to say that when I got to the sixties (I don't mean in age, I mean the decade) I began to realise that there were other Christians who

had one perspective on a truly Biblical understanding of the Christian life which I had almost totally lacked. That was, I had become pietistic to the exclusion of political and social action, and of battling for justice. Yet I cannot see how we as Christians can communicate to people that we are concerned for the whole of their being if we are drawing back at that point. Neither can I understand those whose concern seems to be only for social and political involvement, albeit in the name of Christ, but not for seeking to help people to discover the solution to that greatest need – the knowledge of God's forgiveness and love in their lives. If I were offered one thing as a result of this Assembly, it would be that we might have an end to that divide.[18]

Despite the achievements of the National Assembly, questions were raised before and after the event regarding the future of the NIE. The Council of Reference discussed this in February 1980. Donald's response to the questions was: 'We are not concerned for ourselves. Each of us would have an easier lifestyle if we were not members of the Initiative Committee. But we thought that we had the support of the Churches in a long term search for something new in the will of God in this country'.[19] Unity was not, however, achieved, and on 26 January 1981 Donald wrote that the advantage gained at Nottingham was being lost because of discussions about the future of NIE. He felt that the NIE Committee had tried to share its enthusiasm with the Council of Reference, but largely without success. He was also concerned that the Church of England representatives on the Council referred everything back to the Church of England Board for Mission and Unity. Donald was clearly frustrated that little progress was being made

---

[18] Closing Address at the NIE Conference, Nottingham, September 1980.

[19] Whitehead and Sneddon, *An Unwanted Child?*, p. 36.

and considered that advances could not be made unless the NIE had freedom.[20]

Donald's hopes were not to be realised. He set out what he saw as the achievements of the NIE: united prayer; shared evangelism; county support groups for evangelism; theological formulations; the census 'Prospects for the Nineties', which gave an overall picture of church attendance (showing a drop below 10 per cent); the Nottingham Assembly with 900 Christians from widely divergent backgrounds who worshipped and studied together; and the development of special interest groups at the National Assembly, which looked at the urban poor, unemployment and other faiths. Donald put forward a series of options regarding the future of the NIE. An option that Donald did not wish to see was the one that was chosen. David Taylor's work was brought to an end. Donald wrote to express his disappointment to Tom Houston, Executive Director of the Bible Society. Houston's own perspective was that apart from Donald English no new leaders had emerged in evangelism.

There was widespread recognition of Donald English as a national ecumenical church leader as a result of his NIE work. Bernard Thorogood, General Secretary of the URC, wrote: 'I thought that the use of the gifts of Donald English would be a key factor for the next two year programme. So I wrote to Kenneth Greet [Secretary of the Methodist Conference] to ask whether Donald could be released from a full programme at the college in order to concentrate on NIE. The reply was negative.' The EA also had ideas about Donald as an 'ambassador at large' for a limited period. Donald had, however, been appointed General Secretary of the Home Mission Division and it was impossible for

---

[20] D. English to the Chairman and Vice-Chairman of the Council of Reference of the NIE, 26 January 1981.

him to fulfil an ecumenical role at the same time as assuming his new Methodist responsibilities.[21]

One of the long-lasting results of the NIE was that Canon Derek Palmer was asked as Home Secretary of the Church of England Board of Mission and Unity to take up the idea of creating an ecumenical organisation that would deal with enquiries from TV, radio and press advertising. Palmer writes:

> I found this very hard, as there was still very little real commitment to putting resources into any organisation that was not still mainly denominational. But one Church leader threw his weight behind it and without Donald English there would be no Christian Enquiry Agency [CEA] at work today. He not only gave me, as its first Chairman great personal support and advice and turned up at meetings to show it, but he also persuaded the Methodist Church to put some much-needed finance into the project ... The subsequent history of CEA shows how farsighted Donald was, and although it has always been very under funded it has proved and under Jeff Bonser is again showing what a useful tool it can be in the service of ecumenical evangelism.

This is exactly what Donald would have wanted.

*   *   *   *   *

In spite of the demise of the NIE in 1983, Donald's own ecumenical work continued. The British Council of Churches Evangelism Committee to some degree took over NIE's work. Brian Beck writes:

---

[21] Paper by D. English, 'A Future for NIE?', 1981; D. English to T. Houston, 22 March 1982; Whitehead and Sneddon, *An Unwanted Child?*, pp. 42–3.

Donald was seen as the only person who could carry the confidence and support of others (particularly the evangelical
constituency) into the new structures. Similarly, when the BCC
gave way to Churches Together in England [CTE], Donald was
asked to chair the CTE Co-ordinating Group for Evangelisation. It was in this latter phase that he made what some ecumenical partners saw as his one major slip-up. Since the work of
the Group for Evangelisation was increasing it was suggested
that a member of the Group should be appointed as part-time
paid Executive Secretary. Donald proposed this appointment
from the chair and it was agreed; but when it was reported to the
CTE Enabling Group there was great consternation that such
action had been taken without reference to them and (to quote
the then General Secretary of CTE) 'all hell was let loose'. The
matter was soon amicably resolved, however ... Mistake or no,
[Donald's] leadership continued to be widely appreciated, a
further token of which was his invitation to serve as Moderator
of the Free Church Federal Council during the year 1986–87.

Roger Whitehead was appointed as the Executive Secretary
of the CTE Group for Evangelisation and worked with
Donald, the Chair of the Group. In 1994, when Donald
handed over his role as Chair, he urged churches not to be
satisfied with the fringes of church life but to take on the
issues of the day which concerned ordinary people, from
war and ecology to the advances in embryology. He argued
that a church centred not in itself but within the community
would encourage and equip experts who were Christians to
be its spokespersons, and it would help individuals and
families and wider communities to be themselves. Donald
was never content simply to be ecumenical. For him the
wider purpose was always mission. Appropriately, Whitehead thanked Donald not only for his work as Chair of the
CTE Group, which reflected the breadth of NIE, but for his

close involvement in 'ecumenical evangelisation' from 1976, the date when he began his involvement in the NIE.[22]

Alongside his wider ecumenical involvement Donald was committed to the work of drawing together the Free Churches. From 1986 to 1987, as Moderator of the Free Church Federal Council, he raised the question for the consideration of Free Church leaders as to whether or not there were any such things as 'Free Church principles' any longer. He acknowledged that some were arguing that the various Christian denominations were now happily learning from one another and adapting to hitherto unfamiliar attitudes and activities. Distinctions that had relevance in the past were therefore no longer valid. Donald agreed that Christians were widening their horizons and changing some of their attitudes. He was grateful for all that was being shared across the denominations. This did not necessarily mean, however, that it was now no longer appropriate to speak of Free Church principles. On the matter of the role of the laity, Donald compared the limited part played by lay people in Anglican worship to the fact that in Methodism 75 per cent of Sunday services were the total responsibility of lay people. The role of the elder in the United Reformed Church, or the deacon in a Baptist Church, he argued, also reflected a very deeply significant principle of the way in which lay people share in the ministry of the Free Churches. He also stressed the heritage of the Free Churches as champions of the poor and the needy.[23]

Throughout his time as Free Church Moderator, Donald kept social issues to the fore. His personal notes show the themes he addressed. He supported sanctions against South Africa in an attempt to bring apartheid to an end, arguing that the slow, patient way of negotiation sometimes did not

---

[22] Minutes of a Meeting of the Churches' Co-ordinating Group for Evangelisation, 13 June 1994.

[23] Free Church Moderator's notes, 1987.

make any advance if there was a stubborn resistance to fundamental change. The majority of black people in South Africa, he argued, would evidently rather be free eventually even at the price of unemployment rather than work under such oppression. A not wholly unrelated issue to which Donald gave attention during his year as moderator was that of the black-majority churches in the UK. He was encouraged by the conversations going on with the Afro-West Indian United Council of Christian Churches. 'Our black brothers and sisters', said Donald, 'speak to us out of much disappointment and pain at their treatment in this country.' As he saw it, black people did not simply wish to be part of the various systems; they wished to be able to re-shape the systems so that they might more fairly and truly meet the needs they felt. These things would not happen at once, said Donald, even within the church, but that should not stop the churches from dreaming and working towards a more ideal situation.

During an address he gave to the Free Church Federal Council annual lunch in March 1987,[24] Donald returned to the theme of Free Church identity. Speaking to an audience that included as guests the Archbishop of York and the Arch-bishop of Westminster, Donald argued that each Christian had a denominational heritage of immense value and he commended what he called 'exuberant denominationalism'. By this he did not, he insisted, mean sectarianism or isola-tionism. Rather he considered that in the present 'untidy situ-ation' each denomination should explore the riches it had inherited, to test its deepest meaning and its continuing rele-vance. 'I hope', he said, 'we are past the days of playing down what we are, in order to get on with others who are equally playing down what they are.' He did not see 'lowest common denominator' Christianity as an appropriate basis for unity.

[24] Free Church Federal Council Annual Lunch, Connaught Rooms, 19 March 1987.

At the same time, Donald did not believe everything inherited by a tradition was necessarily valuable. He suggested that part of the process of addressing a denominational heritage was to face the pain of recognising that some things were obsolete.

In the same address Donald argued strongly for the need for sharing across denominational boundaries. This part of his address could have been given to any audience and was not confined to the work of the Free Churches. He spoke of some of the unexpected events that had taken place. 'Who would have thought', he said, using one example, 'that charismatic renewal would have begun in the American Episcopal Church, and that having begun it would have spread right across our denominations?' He argued that it was probably necessary 'if we are to move towards spirituality, service and mission which is both relevant to the late twentieth century and entirely effective in achieving what it aims to do' for traditional ways to change. He set out for consideration the balancing of different styles – altar-centred worship, pulpit-centred worship and pew-centred worship. Continuing on this note, Donald suggested that churches needed to be ready for a 'certain untidiness'. He illustrated this with reference to the recent decision by the Church of England to ordain women. This would make one set of ecumenical relations more difficult but another set easier. Finally, Donald returned to the theme of mission, always close to his heart. He viewed many discussions about church union as self-centred and made a powerful plea for working together in mission.

In this area, Donald saw the ecumenical process entitled 'Not Strangers but Pilgrims', which would issue in 'Churches Together', as a cause of satisfaction. He applauded the ecumenical small groups that were operating. This was in line with Donald's deep concern that the churches ought to be coming together, not for the purposes of some organised scheme, but for the purpose of truly being the people of God in the world. His hope was that as the churches in the later 1980s moved towards what was called a 'New Ecumenical Instrument' the Free Church contribution would be a responsible and effective one. At the same time as believing that denominations needed to be less concerned about themselves and more concerned about the expression of God's love to the world, Donald also believed that there were things within the Free Churches – their history, their convictions, their perspectives on models of leadership and on church organisation – which were rightly recognised by others as significant.

These remarks by Donald became a matter for discussion. Bernard Thorogood of the URC wrote to Donald to query the phrase 'exuberant denominationalism'. For him it suggested a return to the 1930s when denominations were seeking the limelight to push their special points of view. Thorogood agreed with Donald that denominations had gifts to share. 'I cannot', he said, 'run away from our understanding of eldership any more than you can throw away the Circuit!' But Thorogood suggested that there was wisdom in Lesslie Newbigin's critique that 'denominationalism largely derives from, and also serves, an individualist view of faith that is not primary for the Kingdom'. In his response, Donald affirmed his belief that denominational boundaries and barriers were being broken down, but suggested that the reason why denominationalism would 'not in the end do is not because theologically it feeds off our individualism, but because pragmatically it divides us from one another when we all need each other so desperately in order to bring proper worship to God and effective mission to the world'. Donald believed that the danger of Newbigin's critique was that it did not acknowledge sufficiently the way in which God's sovereignty had worked out in denominational history.[25] In

---

[25] B.G. Thorogood to D. English, 20 March 1987; D. English to B.G. Thorogood, 31 March 1987.

much of their ecumenical thinking, however, Bernard Thorogood and Donald were at one.

If Donald was concerned to explore the problems and opportunities of ecumenical dialogue and co-operation, what about dialogue with other faiths? This is a different topic, and one to which Donald did not give nearly as much attention as he did to Christians coming together, but it was something to which, in his typically wide-ranging way, he did give thought. It is well known that engaging with the issues raised by inter-faith dialogue is not always easy for evangelicals. Yet in this area Donald was always open to exploration. John Newton recalls that Donald appreciated a paper by the Roman Catholic Michael Evans on 'Evangelism and Non-Christians'. Newton himself was working on this subject within Methodism, and produced a leaflet on 'Evangelism and Other Faiths'. Newton recalls a conversation with Donald in which Donald thanked him for what he had written on other faiths, indicating that it was what he would want to say. This is not to suggest that Donald was in any way wishing to dilute the evangelical commitment to witness to all people, including those of other faiths, but rather that he recognised the great challenge to witness in a sensitive way in a multi-faith society.

*   *   *   *   *

In his appraisal of Donald's ministry, Brian Beck described him as a comprehensive man, one who was always a committed evangelical, but who at the same time was never narrow. This was the approach Donald brought to his ecumenical involvement. It is significant that Donald explained to the NIE Assembly in 1980 that it was in the 1960s (when he was in his thirties and his horizons were broadening through his time in Africa) that he began to realise that there were other Christians who had perspectives on the

Christian life that he lacked. It was this broadening that enabled Donald to be an ecumenical enthusiast. Yet in all his thinking Donald remained an evangelist. He was concerned for inter-faith dialogue but his proclamation of the uniqueness of Christ was central to his ministry. Brian Beck notes that he was committed to and active in the ecumenical movement as someone steeped in Methodist traditions and a strong advocate for the Free Church heritage and Free Church way of life, but someone who was equally at home with Anglicans and Roman Catholics. In this significant area Donald was both a Methodist and more than a Methodist.

9

International Ministry

Donald English burst upon the World Methodist scene while he was still a tutor at Wesley College, Bristol. If anyone who did not know the story asked him in later years how it happened, he said: 'My involvement in World Methodism all began with a chap called Peter Bolt!' The details are of interest. Peter Bolt was a British Methodist minister who was also Secretary of the Programme Committee for the World Methodist Conference being held in Dublin in the summer of 1976. He had heard Donald giving expository Bible studies some time previously and had been greatly impressed. When the committee came to discuss names for a Bible study speaker for the Dublin conference, therefore, Peter said: 'I've got just the man – Donald English.' There were blank looks from the rest of the committee, made up of international representatives from different branches of World Methodism. 'Donald English? Who's he? Nobody's ever heard of him!' Some wanted a well-known name, others wanted a speaker from a Third World country, but Peter pressed his case and the committee eventually – if somewhat apprehensively – agreed.

They need not have worried. Donald's four Bible studies on 'A Day of Mission' (Isaiah 45:18–25), 'A Day of Understanding' (Hebrews 1:1–4), 'A Day of God's Power' (Acts 4:23–31) and 'A Day of Brotherhood' (Luke 10:25–37) proved outstandingly popular, and the fact that these early morning studies attracted increasingly large audiences was testimony in itself to his unique personality and gifts. One of the British ministers attending the conference, Brian Greet, wrote: 'He held us spellbound with a crystal clear exposition informed by a scholarly grasp of the text and context and lit up by a scintillating wit.' The final session ended with a standing ovation, and the official record of the conference proceedings described the studies as 'four widely acclaimed Conference Bible Studies ... a highlight of the Thirteenth World Methodist Conference'. Donald's place in the life of World Methodism was never in doubt thereafter. Although he had previously been known only in Britain and Nigeria, Methodists from many other countries took him to their hearts and recognised him as a natural leader. Dr Joe Hale, who was elected General Secretary of the World Methodist Council at that conference, later commented:

> I have never known another instance of a person being literally thrust upon the world stage so forcefully, and in just one week through a single event. His Bible Studies in Dublin made him a world figure virtually overnight, and opened doors to a world where he would be received gladly and with enormous respect, not simply for his speaking ability and winsome personality but also for the content of his message and the character of his life.[1]

That Dublin conference provided a foretaste of the global contribution Donald was destined to make over the next two decades and more.

The fact that only three years later Asbury Theological Seminary in the USA awarded Donald an honorary degree

---

[1] See also J. Hale, 'Donald English, the World Leader' in Abbott (ed.), *Donald English*, pp. 29–31.

provides ample evidence of the rapid spread of his reputation to America. In the spring of 1980 he was invited to give a series of Bible studies at the Southern Asia Bishops' retreat-cum-conference held at the Cathedral Church of the Redemption in Delhi, India, with bishops attending not only from India itself but also Pakistan, Bangladesh and Sri Lanka. Later that same year Peter Bolt again pressed Donald into action, this time as Bible study speaker at the first World Methodist International Christian Youth Conference held in Truro, Cornwall, which attracted over a thousand young people from forty-seven nations. Paul Nsubuga from Uganda (one of twelve Ugandans attending – most of whom were later murdered under Idi Amin) wrote to Donald after the event to thank him:

> Whenever I try to think of our conference my memory first gives me your picture, how you used to teach in a way which I can't explain to anybody, and I remember your sympathy for we people who came from Uganda. Now when reading the Bible I always use the guidelines which you taught us.

In July 1981, only five years after his first exposure to World Methodism, Donald was elected to the eight-member Presidium (the small group responsible with the officers for leading the affairs of the World Methodist Council [WMC] between meetings) at the WMC Centennial Council in Honolulu, Hawaii. That same conference also saw Donald's first involvement with the work of World Methodism's evangelism ministry, and in particular the formation of the World Evangelism Institute. Two evangelism seminars had already been run in 1978 and 1979 by Candler School of Theology, Emory University, Georgia, USA, under the leadership of George Morris (a professor at Candler), Joe Hale (WMC General Secretary) and Alan Walker (WMC Director of Evangelism), and this gave rise to the idea of a World Evangelism

Institute to be run as a co-operative ministry by Emory University and the WMC. Alan Walker included a formal proposal to that end in his written report for the Honolulu council meeting, including the following suggestions:

1. Ministers and lay people would be brought from across the world for short and longer courses.
2. The World Evangelism Institute staff would go at intervals to different countries to teach evangelism for a period.
3. Teaching resources such as audio-visuals, tapes and books would be developed for use by the churches.

When the proposal was moved, however, Trevor Rowe of the British delegation rose to oppose it as what he called 'evangelical imperialism'. 'The task for the World Methodist Council', he insisted, 'is to support evangelism in each place, not to do it. What the world supremely needs is the good news that the poor can bring – a message they alone can bring to many of us.' After some animated and at times heated debate Donald English rose to say it had not been easy for Trevor Rowe to say what he had, and that he (Donald) found himself in a minority in the British group, most of whom shared Rowe's concerns. He hoped the council would 'find a way in which the momentum of the World Evangelism programme could be continued and the questions being raised from England or anywhere else could go on being raised and answered'. Institute meetings should take place in different parts of the world, not just the USA; instead of producing large amounts of literature in English from a central office, money might be given to churches around the world to produce material in their own language; and effort should be put into learning lessons from around the world which could fashion the plans and policies of the World Evangelism programme. Donald's amendments to the proposal were carried by an overwhelming vote, and great appreciation was expressed for his ability to turn a potentially divisive encounter into something quite positive.

George Morris, who became the Evangelism Institute's first Director, observes:

> Donald English played a strategic role in the early development of the World Methodist Evangelism Institute. Its strategy and theology held great appeal for him, and when he was asked to serve on the first Institute committee he gladly agreed. His contribution was highly significant and his influence continues to live on in its world-wide ministry. Not only did he help in its formation, but he was also a valued participant on the faculties of both Regional and International Seminars. Much of the success of the Institute is a tribute to Donald English.

The First International Seminar run by the World Evangelism Institute was held at Emory University in the summer of 1982. Delegates attended from all over the world, and the faculty included lecturers from Mexico, Kenya, Singapore, Australia, the USA and Britain. Donald gave a series of lectures on the doctrines of creation and redemption as they relate to evangelism, insisting that both doctrines must be held in creative tension if the church was to engage in truly holistic evangelism. He said:

> Creation *and* redemption must be the basis of our Christianity. There is continuity between the world and the gospel, between nature and grace, between culture and the life of the church. If we leave ourselves only with a creation basis for our message we will never get people into the Kingdom. But if we are concerned only with a redemption-based evangelism we are starting too far down the line for most people to hear us. Jesus started where the people were. I am a theologian not of the either/or, but of the both/and.

After speaking at the Fifth International Seminar, held at Cliff College, Donald wrote to George Morris:

> Almost 150 people from all around the world were obviously having a deeply meaningful experience. The combination of fellowship and worship, serious study and personal commitment to evangelism was very striking. The concern to be enthusiastic about evangelism whilst retaining rigorous academic standards makes the Institute unique around the world in terms of preparing evangelists.

A subsequent letter said: 'I believe that the Institute is one of the finest pieces of Christian work happening anywhere in the world at the moment.' Indeed, Methodism is the only Christian world communion to have such a body devoted to evangelism.

Marking the fifteenth anniversary of the founding of the Institute in 1996, Eddie Fox (who succeeded Sir Alan Walker as World Director of Evangelism in 1989) recorded: 'In the past fifteen years 3,000 persons have been trained in evangelism in more than thirty Seminars through the ministry of the World Methodist Evangelism Institute.' He went on to note that:

> Donald was chosen by World Evangelism to serve in the initial group of Regional Secretaries. He met with them at their first international meeting in London in 1988 and was always present at each subsequent gathering. He lectured at World Evangelism Institute Seminars on many occasions. When Donald spoke, people listened. He was powerful in his leadership, yet gentle in all his relationships. He stood alongside other world leaders in evangelism in the challenge to the Methodist movement to be faithful to our heritage and reason for being. By precept and example he clearly changed the course of World Methodism in his two decades of leadership.

Nowhere was Donald's evangelistic ministry appreciated more than in the USA. To mark its fortieth anniversary, in 1989, the Foundation for Evangelism of the United Methodist Church decided to select forty evangelists from the Methodist world, both living and dead, for recognition as having achieved unusual distinction. The list included world-renowned figures like E. Stanley Jones, John R. Mott, D.T. Niles and W.E. Sangster – and Donald English. In the event he was unable to attend the ceremony, and wrote to Bishop Earl G. Hunt: 'Sadly I will not be able to be present. Perhaps appropriately, I am preaching across that weekend down in Cornwall. I have a feeling that John Wesley would have preferred me to be preaching in Cornwall rather than receiving an award in North Carolina!'

* * * * *

Whilst evangelism was a priority close to his heart, it was by no means Donald English's only concern. He was a man of wide interests, and his growing international work involved him in a variety of other activities – social, political and ecumenical. Having previously served as a missionary in Nigeria, he was delighted in 1985 to be given the opportunity to represent British Methodism (by then as ex-President of the Conference) at an extremely important ceremony taking place in that country. Since Donald's time in Nigeria in the 1960s there had been growing discord in Nigerian Methodism, leading to a major split following the adoption of a new constitution in 1976 (albeit with 118 votes in favour, 1 against and 0 neutral). This had involved a series of changes that were largely ecclesiastical rather than doctrinal, among them the change of name of the Methodist President to Patriarch, the introduction of archbishops, bishops, presbyters and priests, and the wearing of ecclesiastical robes. There were charges that the Patriarch had become monarchical and autocratic, and the last straw for some was a move in 1982 to make the Patriarch's office a lifetime appointment. Divisions had escalated between the former Eastern Nigeria District and its Western counterpart and the divisions began to develop tribal overtones. As a memorandum from one group of Methodists put it:

> Our people reject the Patriarchal system completely. It has taken the Methodist Church Nigeria, all too unwillingly, into the Eastern Orthodox Church with the wearing of crowns, diadems, gorgeous robes and rings and the carrying around of keys and crosses ... Our people are all for the return to the simple but dignified clerical attire of old.

Proposals to change the long-held tradition that the head of the church should always come from the West (where Methodism was older and had many more members) and the Secretary of Conference from the East caused further upset. Church services were disturbed and no less than eighteen lawsuits were initiated.

Kenneth Greet, as Chair of the World Methodist Council, sent a small delegation to attempt reconciliation. Although their work did not bear immediate fruit, a contribution was made to the eventual healing. Against the background of severe tension, it was remarkable that the event Donald English was invited to attend on 20 and 21 January 1985 took place at all. It was a full weekend. Saturday saw the consecration and investiture of bishops, at which Donald preached, and the Sunday service included both the investiture of the Rt. Revd Sunday Mbang (one of Donald's former students at Umuahia) as the new Patriarch and the integration of Christ Church Methodist Zion Church Nigeria Incorporated into the Methodist Church, Nigeria. Sunday Mbang would later become Chair of the World

Methodist Council. These meetings in January 1985 represented an important step towards reconciliation in Nigeria. Donald later described them in his report to the President of the British Methodist Conference, Gordon Barritt, as follows:

> In terms of symbolism, ritual movement and general colour these services far surpassed anything we ever attempted. They were also somewhat longer! Saturday's service began at 10.00 am and finished at 3.30pm. On Sunday we began at 10.30am and finished at 5.15pm. Both of these were continuous services without any break, so I have some news for my congregations next Sunday!
>
> The context was not without its difficulties. On the day before the investiture of bishops there was a court case brought by some people in the West for an injunction against the investiture on the grounds that the system was not a proper Methodist one. This was dismissed because nominations had been made in late September and the objectors had waited until this weekend to bring their case. There is still, of course, the '1962 Conference' group in the East. There were lots of police there just to make sure that law and order was kept, but there was not any difficulty in that way at all ... There must have been about 2,000 to 3,500 there on the Sunday. When the Secretary of the Conference declared 'We have a new Patriarch' there was a deafening and joyous shout of 'Hallelujah!' Trumpeters in the gallery from the Boys' Brigade played a fanfare and the entire congregation broke into a Yoruba melody, with words that mean: 'What we thought would be very difficult, God has done for us easily'. The new Patriarch is very concerned to heal the wounds in the Methodist body in Nigeria, and a good start was made with the reception of the Christ Methodist Zion Church Nigeria Incorporated.[2]

---

[2] Letter dated 24 January 1985.

Tensions of a very different sort were the focus of another invitation to Donald in November of that same year, 1985, this time to give two major addresses in Dublin at an Anglo-Irish conference on the role of the churches in British–Irish relationships. Donald's Irish connections through Bertha meant that he had taken an increasingly active interest in the Irish situation, and he was well qualified to speak, being at the same time involved in the situation yet detached from it. The hundred or so participants in the conference included not only representatives of the churches, both clergy and laity, but others from different walks of life (including the press and politics), such as Clifford Longley, James Naughtie, Gerald Priestland and Mary Robinson. Donald's aim was to help them to explore the seemingly intractable historical position through theological reflection and the use of biblical models for handling complex and difficult situations and relationships.

The following year, 1986, saw the Fifteenth World Methodist Conference in Nairobi, Kenya, on the theme 'Christ Jesus: God's "Yes" for the World'. Uniquely, Donald English was invited to give the conference Bible studies again. Over 2,500 people were present from over 90 countries and were welcomed by the President of the Republic of Kenya, His Excellency Daniel arap Moi. Other speakers included Lord Tonypandy (Britain), Desmond Tutu (South Africa) and Charles ('Chuck') Colson (USA). Donald himself had flown through the night from London in order to be there for the first of his Bible studies, and explained his reason for coming late to the conference: 'I was taking part in a little local ceremony we had in England yesterday, with about 300 million people watching over our shoulders.' He was referring to the wedding of Prince Andrew and Sarah Ferguson in Westminster Abbey! A report of Donald's Bible studies in *World Parish*, the journal of the World Methodist Council, said:

The Bible Study each morning was a central part of the conference. Beginning with a passage from the book of Colossians Dr English urged all world powers to heed the fact that, according to St Paul, all 'thrones, dominions, principalities or powers' were created by God and for God. The choice of Dr English to lead the conference Bible Studies was in itself remarkable in that he is the only person in the 105-year history of the World Methodist Council to [lead the studies twice], the first occasion being studies ten years ago at the Thirteenth Conference in Ireland.

It was during this 1986 Conference that Donald was elected Vice-Chair of the World Methodist Council, strengthening the likelihood of his being elected Chair at the end of that quinquennium when the Conference next gathered.

World Methodist Conferences debate a wide variety of issues, and a topic high on the agenda in Nairobi was the situation in South Africa. The debate ended with a series of resolutions calling upon Methodists around the world to pray and work for an end to the system of apartheid in that country, and the compilation of a list of five requests to the South African government. These were to:

1. Unconditionally release Nelson Mandela and other political prisoners and detainees.
2. Lift the State of Emergency and end the violence and loss of life in the townships.
3. Provide integrated educational opportunities for all regardless of race or colour.
4. Abolish immediately the apartheid system and repeal the Population Registration Act.
5. Begin negotiations by representatives of all South African peoples for a political and economic future in which all participate with equal rights.

A final decision was that the World Methodist Council should send a delegation to South Africa to express pastoral solidarity with its suffering people and convey Methodism's concerns to all parties. After a long delay, the President of the Republic of South Africa, P.W. Botha, agreed to meet a delegation in Capetown on 10 November 1987, and Donald English, as Vice-Chairman, was one of those chosen to go. This was the first delegation from a major world denomination to visit in this way. In his letter to Joe Hale, the WMC General Secretary, President Botha said that the 'proposed delegation should try to spend enough time in South Africa to form a balanced view of the country' and offered to make suggestions 'about whom and what they should see'.

Donald's own report of the visit in *DSR News*, a paper published by the British Methodist Church's Division of Social Responsibility,[3] describes something of what they saw:

> We met church leaders, groups of ordained and lay Methodists, black and white. We worshipped with, spoke to, listened to, congregations black and mixed. We went to Soweto, Crossroads, Alexandra, Khayelitshe, Anfervacht. We stayed in Johannesburg, Capetown and Bloemfontein. We heard testimony from young people recently released from detention, adults just out of prison, black and white Christians who had been detained or imprisoned for long periods of time. We met Govan Mbeki, released from prison while we were there.
>
> We spent time in conversation with Winnie Mandela who impressed us as a dignified, wise and passionately committed person. She told us that of the 27 years in which her husband had been imprisoned, only the last 18 months had been 'contact' visits. For over twenty years she had not even been allowed to touch him. She said she believed we were right in visiting President Botha, and when asked what we should tell him replied, 'Get the soldiers and security police out of schools

[3] *DSR News*, Spring 1988.

and townships, and let us get on with our life and education.'
One of the group asked her how she managed to keep going
over such a long period. She replied, 'I hear the sound of the
footsteps of the nation behind me.'

We met black leaders in the townships, those with the confidence of the blacks rather than those appointed by the government. We visited housing schemes, training centres, a gold
mine and a black children's graveyard which I will never forget
as long as I live.

The meeting with the State President himself was scheduled
to last for forty-five minutes, but in the event went on for
two-and-a-quarter hours. The leader of the delegation was
Bishop Lawi Imathiu from Kenya (Chair of the World
Methodist Council), and besides Donald the group included Joe Hale, three other senior WMC officers (all, as it
happened, Americans – one black and two white) and four
senior leaders of the Methodist Church in South Africa.
Donald's own notes on the meeting give a full and detailed
account of all that was said and done, and begin:

> We were not kept waiting very long, and after photographs,
> were taken through to a room with a large horseshoe shaped
> table. The State President had with him his Parliamentary
> Private Secretary and the Head of Intelligence. He invited Lawi
> to sit next to him, but we had been warned about that and
> Lawi chose to sit further up the table where he could look the
> President in the eye.

After what Donald described as 'a very deep and moving
prayer' led by the President of the South African Methodist
Conference, Lawi Imathiu was invited to speak. He said
they had not come as politicians, nor had they come to tell
the President how to run his government, but to reflect the
deep conviction of fifty-four million Methodist people

around the world that all men and women are created in the image of God and are entitled to be treated as members of God's human family. Donald was then called upon to present the five requests agreed at the Nairobi conference and explain the reasoning behind them. President Botha was courteous but very tough. He listened carefully, taking notes of what was said, and then replied in detail and at length (some fifty-five minutes), rereading the five requests one by one and each time saying 'No' and explaining his reasons. After his response he clearly wanted to end the conversation, but Lawi protested that he should at least hear what the South Africans in the group had to say. Botha seemed to like Lawi, saying: 'We're Africans. We can talk and understand each other' (a barely veiled reference to what he saw as 'outside interference' by Britain and America), and allowed him to keep the meeting going.

What did the meeting achieve? Donald wrote after the visit:

> My reflection on it is that we did what we had gone to do, namely we presented our resolutions forcefully and did not back down on any of them in the face of his speech by way of reply. I think he was touched by the Christian approach, and must have taken note of the fact that we represented such a large world communion, not sponsored by particular nations. The visit attracted a large amount of publicity in South Africa, with major newspapers giving reports and editorial to the event.

It had been what Lawi Imathiu called 'a difficult and depressing meeting'. Yet, as he put it: 'It takes many cuts to fell a tree, and you never know which chop will finally fell it.'

On his return home Donald wrote a personal letter to President Botha thanking him for having received the delegation, but forthrightly saying:

We were naturally disappointed that your response to our resolutions was not more positive ... My hope and prayer continues to be that your negative response does not reflect your whole attitude to us and what we were pleading for. We came out of genuine concern for all the people in South Africa, and we hope our visit communicated that to you.[4]

* * * * *

The following year, 1988, saw Donald concerned with more domestic affairs back in Britain, although it was a significant year for World Methodism, marking 250 years since John Wesley's conversion experience in Aldersgate Street, London. Writing in *World Parish*, Joe Hale observed: 'May 24, 1738, give or take a few months, is the birthday of world Methodism.' Special celebratory services and other events were held all over Britain and around the world, the major one being a service in St Paul's Cathedral, London, attended by Her Majesty the Queen and Prince Philip. Donald English was invited to be the preacher, and his sermon addressed the need to live life on a deeper level. Represented in the congregation, he said, were Christian brothers and sisters from around the world for whom living as Christians involved constant personal risk, in whom the experience of Christ was not additional to the rest of life but fundamental to its substance. The basic question, he said, had been put by an American visitor to the British Methodist Conference in 1978: 'What is it about your life which it takes Jesus Christ to explain?' Following the service the Queen's Secretary wrote to the President of the Methodist Conference, William R. Davies, saying:

I write at the Queen's command to thank you for inviting her and the Duke of Edinburgh to attend the service commemorating

[4] Letter dated 15 December 1987.

the 250th anniversary of the conversion of John Wesley. Her Majesty and His Royal Highness were delighted to be part of your huge congregation. The memory of John Wesley was indeed well served by the assembled choirs and congregation, and by the words of the sermon by Dr English.

The first few months of 1989 brought a welcome sabbatical period for Donald English, and from the February until the end of April he and Bertha lived in an apartment at Candler School of Theology, Emory University, in Atlanta, Georgia. Although that period afforded plenty of time for relaxation it was by no means all leisure. Donald was variously described as 'Visiting Professor' and 'Churchman in Residence', and taught two periods from 8.00am to 9.20am each week on the theology and practice of Christian mission for students doing masters' and doctoral degrees. He also preached in the college chapel and various local churches, and wrote 50,000 words of his commentary on Mark's Gospel, subsequently published by Tyndale Press. Professor George Morris, at whose invitation Donald and Bertha had gone to Candler, remembers that 'students queued up in order to get into Donald's classes, and those privileged to study with him still sing his praises'.

May 1990 brought yet more world travelling for Donald and Bertha, this time to Hong Kong, to attend the annual conference of the Methodist Church there. Besides the sessions of the conference itself, however, there was opportunity to engage in plenty of sightseeing to places like The Peak, the Portuguese province of Macau and the Dragon Boat Festival at Tuen Mun, and to visit schools, refugee communities and local Chinese churches. One visit that particularly impressed Donald was to Hang Fook Camp, one of the centres run by Jackie Pullinger. Having read about her work and seen it featured on television he and Bertha were keen to see it for themselves. Jackie Pullinger had gone out to Hong Kong from Croydon, not far from the Englishes' home in Cheam, to teach music, but had soon been drawn into working with drug addicts and others. Donald wrote:

> It really is most impressive, particularly when the man who showed us round was so presentable and articulate, but had actually been on heroin for fifteen years, being totally freed of it six years ago. His testimony to the power of Jesus was most moving, as was that of an old lady who had been on drugs and a prostitute since her early teens, but having been found as a street person was totally released from drugs and prostitution, and now does much of the laundry at the camp we visited.

Two particular commitments in Hong Kong were to deliver Bible studies on two passages in Mark's Gospel. Donald records with typical enthusiasm:

> All the speaking was by interpretation, and it was interesting to be back in that way of speech after the years in Nigeria. It's a curious feeling, because there's no such thing as a flow of sentences into paragraphs! The meetings were very well attended, and the congregation was composed very largely of young people and young couples. A good number of them were taking notes. It was such a privilege to be in Hong Kong. Bertha and I both felt that it was one of the most memorable weeks in our life.

Only a month or so after returning from the Far East, and following his induction as President of the Methodist Conference for the second time, Donald flew out to join a group of pilgrims from the Caribbean, Mexico, the USA and Britain who were visiting ancient sites in the Middle East and focusing on the task of contemporary Christian apologetics. Visiting places like Nicea (where the Nicene Creed was formulated in AD 325), Corinth, Ephesus and Constantinople, they enjoyed a programme of nine lectures and engaged in worship as well as exploring these historic sites. Eddie Fox, World Director of Evangelism, spoke in the arena where the Apostle Paul's preaching incited the Ephesians to riot, Geoffrey Wainwright addressed the group in the fifth-century Constantinople church where the Second Ecumenical Council (381) had set out a clear doctrine of the Holy Spirit, and Donald English gave the final presentation in the lecture series on 'Christian Apologetics – What are We to Do?' He affirmed apologetics as the task of 'clearing away the problems and obstacles that keep people from believing' and warned that it is not accommodating the Christian faith to the latest fad or seeking to make it fit the culture. It was this lecture that put apologetics on the agenda of World Methodism. He concluded: 'If the Christian church loses the battle for the mind we will never win the battle for the soul.'

1990 also saw Donald back in South Africa for a second important visit. By now F.W. de Klerk had succeeded P.W. Botha as State President. In view of de Klerk's courageous steps in unbanning the African National Congress and other black political organisations, the release of Nelson Mandela from prison that February and the President's stated intention to bring apartheid to an end, the World Methodist Council thought it an opportune time to make further representations. Again, Bishop Lawi Imathiu led the delegation, and Donald English was a member of the accompanying group, which received a reception that was very different from the first visit.

This meeting took place on 28 August in the Union Buildings, Pretoria, and began with a warm welcome from the State President, who himself suggested that they should open in prayer, which Donald led. Lawi Imathiu expressed his belief that Mr de Klerk had been brought to power in God's time for a particular purpose, and then the Presiding Bishop of the South Africa Methodist Church, Stanley Mogoba, was invited to speak. He believed there was a great tide of goodwill towards what the State President and his government were trying to do, but stressed the need for early action to establish negotiations over a new constitution and the importance of giving more attention to the education of black children. Then it was Donald's turn to speak, and he raised two issues: firstly, the important role the church had to play in negotiations over South Africa's future; and secondly, the President's own perception of what form of power sharing would be appropriate. In a speech earlier that year de Klerk had rejected both partition and majority rule as possible ways forward and suggested a 'home-made variety best suited to South Africa' as the only solution.

The President responded frankly and openly, expressing his belief as a Calvinist that whatever way forward was sought it should pass the test of Bible teaching. He was fully committed to ending apartheid and to the development of a new constitution, and would be glad to respond to further written submissions from the group. Donald noted:

The atmosphere this time was so very different from that of our meeting with State President P.W. Botha in 1987. In that case the door was closed on every request we made. In this case the door seemed to be open in relation to every request we made. It was an encouraging meeting. To say that the way forward is not easy is to be guilty of a massive understatement. But there is also, as far as I am concerned, a tremendous excitement at the possibility of the vindication on the one side of the patience and on the other side the suffering of the black people. I think this visit does justify our last one. We were the more welcome this time because we bothered to come last time.

The way forward was indeed not easy. South Africa continued to experience further disturbance and much violence
over the next few years, with over 6,000 people killed. In
July 1992 Donald wrote a letter to the British Foreign Secretary, Douglas Hurd, and sent a copy to the Prime Minister,
urging that a Commonwealth or UN team should go to
South Africa to monitor the situation; that an international
investigation be conducted into the continuing violence;
that pressure be brought to bear on South Africa to form an
interim government immediately; and that the Commonwealth or the UN should assist in the conduct of free and
fair elections based on universal suffrage as soon as possible.
It was not until May 1994 that Donald was finally able to
write to Bishop Mogoba offering the good wishes of the
Methodist people world-wide as South Africa began a new
era under the leadership of Nelson Mandela as State President. 'The eyes of the world are focused upon South Africa,'
he wrote:

> All of us in the World Methodist Council are aware of the major
> part that the Methodist Church of Southern Africa has played in
> bringing your nation to this moment of new beginning. Others
> have worked alongside you, but you have always been in the
> first line of advance. We stand with you in grateful thanks for
> the faithful and powerful witness you have given. History will
> record your place in the birth of the new South Africa.[5]

By the time he wrote those words, which reflected his deeply
held belief in the important witness of Christian faith in the
world of social and political events, Donald was able to do
so in his capacity as Chair of the World Methodist Council.
His fulfilment of that role is another chapter in the story of
Donald's ministry.

---

[5] Letter dated 9 May 1994.

10

Leading World Methodism

A banner headline on the front page of the *Methodist Recorder* proclaimed 'Donald English Confirmed As New Leader'. The report began:

Twice President of the British Methodist Conference, the Rev Dr Donald English was yesterday presenting the closing message of this 16th World Methodist Conference in Singapore as the new chairperson of the World Methodist Council. Soon after his election as leader of a world Church of more than 54 million people in 90 countries, Dr English told the *Recorder* he felt very inspired at the council meeting at which his nomination was confirmed because of responses which came from Churches such as Liberia, Nigeria, South Africa, Sierra Leone, the Caribbean, South America and Ireland.[1]

It was clear that he enjoyed the confidence and support of Methodists in many continents and nations.

Donald had quickly stamped his leadership on that Singapore conference, and his skills in the chair were widely appreciated. He was passionately concerned to ensure that all points of view were fairly heard, that the smaller and numerically weaker national churches were not overlooked, and that Western ways of doing things were not

[1] *Methodist Recorder*, 1 August 1991.

allowed to dictate the proceedings. Brian Beck, former Secretary of the British Methodist Conference, who was present in Singapore, observed:

> When five hundred church leaders come together from six continents and a dozen different traditions, all born to lead or they wouldn't be there, it's not surprising if the sessions of the Council sometimes resemble a bear garden. But Donald not only exercised a firm hand but made friends of everybody at the same time. He had learned to see things through the eyes of other cultures and understood what things looked like from where they sat.

That was well illustrated by the closing remarks in Donald's address as the newly elected Chair:

> For many of us this will have been a week of considerable frustration; for some of us, not being able to understand all that is said; for others of us, finding that things move much too fast for us to be part of them; for many of us, trying to discover why other people think as they think. The frustration is part of the privilege of belonging to what Dr Wainwright called the symphony with which we praise God. If you want to belong to a group that is all violins, don't come back. Still better, if you only want to play your own violin, you needn't be with anybody and you'll always be right. But if you want to play the symphony in the orchestra of the Lord, you need the rest of us ... We *all* need one another.

As the Singapore conference drew to a close, so Donald English's five years of distinguished leadership as Chair of the World Methodist Council (WMC) began. He made his mark in many different ways. With his concern for good committee administration, he tightened up Council procedures, pressing for agendas and papers to be distributed well ahead of meetings, for a better allocation of time to different aspects of business, and generally for more efficient ways of doing things. More importantly, however, he constantly reminded the Council of its main purpose and vision. Addressing a meeting of the WMC officers at Lake Junaluska, North Carolina, in December 1991, he outlined four things that they needed to keep in mind: they should avoid doing at world level what national and local churches could do, concentrating rather on those central issues that make the Methodist family what it is; they should watch developments at world level and respond to them; they should be seen alongside people suffering and in need; and they should engage in discussion with other major world Christian communions.

Donald's major contribution as World Methodist Chair, however, was not so much in various council and conference meetings as in his continuing travels to different parts of the world. One such visit took place on 26 March 1992 when, together with Joe Hale (WMC General Secretary) and Geoffrey Wainwright (Co-chair of the long-running Methodist–Roman Catholic Dialogue), Donald had a private audience at the Vatican with His Holiness Pope John Paul II. Concerned to observe the correct protocol, Donald asked Joe Hale whether it would be like an audience with Her Majesty the Queen, but was told it would be a much more straightforward affair. The appointed hour arrived and they walked across St Peter's Square, through the great colonnade and into the Vatican, the Swiss Guard snapping to attention as they entered, and began the ascent of the long formal staircase leading the Pope's residence. They passed through a maze of rooms leading to the Pope's library where the audience was to be held and Mgr. Kevin McDonald, a staff member of the Pontifical Council for Promoting Christian Unity and Co-secretary of the Methodist–Catholic Dialogue, explained what would happen: the Pope would greet them individually and then, after they were seated, would make a short presentation, to which Donald would respond. This would be followed by a short time of discussion before a closing exchange of comments and prayers.

It was a memorable experience. If Donald was understandably nervous about it, he need not have worried. In fact, it was the Pope who at one point got things out of sequence, at which Kevin McDonald interjected: 'Your Holiness, we do *this* next!' In his response to the Pope's short address, Donald spoke of Methodism's ongoing commitment to what John Wesley had called 'the catholic spirit', saying: 'In that spirit I warmly give you my hand today.' He went on to refer to two important developments at world level: the new day dawning in South Africa and Eastern Europe, where both the Catholic and Methodist churches had demonstrated their commitment to social action and the struggle for justice; and the common commitment of the two churches, along with others, to a Decade of Evangelisation, pointing especially to the importance of apologetics. 'So often', he concluded, 'we get nearest to one another when together we do the things that Christians should be doing anyway.' The visit to the Pope ended with photographs and an exchange of gifts. The Pope presented Donald with a bound copy of the *Codex Vaticanus*, and Donald in turn gave His Holiness an anthology of Wesley's writings and also a more personal gift – his own recently published commentary on Mark's Gospel.

Whilst at the Vatican Donald also met other Roman Catholic leaders, including Cardinal Edward Idris Cassidy, President of the Pontifical Council for Promoting Christian Unity, with whom he had lunch. These contacts proved valuable in the fulfilment of some of his subsequent responsibilities as WMC Chair. In May 1992, for instance, he received a long letter from Bishop Raul Ruiz Avila, leader of the Methodist Church in Mexico, cataloguing problems that Methodists and other Protestant groups had been experiencing with the Roman Catholic Church since the Pope's recent visit to Mexico, and asking Donald to visit to see the situation for himself. One Mexican Catholic leader had even declared of Protestant churches: 'The sects are like flies, they bother us; but they can never demolish the Roman Catholic Church. That is why they should be driven away.' Donald wrote immediately to Cardinal Cassidy, enclosing details of the matters causing such concern and the specific accusations that had been made. His letter said: 'I am sorry that names are named, but it does seem to me that we will only find the way forward if specific cases are looked into in order to discover how much truth there is in the allegations being made.' He concluded: 'Thank you for opening the possibility of this kind of discussion, painful though it sometimes is. It is a sign that we are truly address-ing the problems which lie in the way of our greater unity, and I am most grateful to God for that.'

* * * * *

The first full WMC Executive Committee meeting Donald chaired took place in Varna, Bulgaria, in September 1992 – interestingly, the place where the last great battle of the Crusades took place in 1444. Those who then believed the sword would prevail had been proved wrong, as also had those atheistic communists who in more recent years had sought to impose their ideas by force. The meetings took place in a venue not far from the Black Sea and near the modern former headquarters of the Communist Party, now Varna's city hall. Local Methodists, persecuted by the communist regime for more than thirty years, greeted members of the Executive with joy and gratitude. It was a significant time, which one observer likened to 'the discovery of long-lost relatives'. 'This is the family to which you belong,' Donald English told them as he waved towards nearly 200 members and guests of the Executive Committee.

Although Methodism had begun in Varna 130 years before, it had been outlawed in the 1960s by the communist authorities, who confiscated buildings and prohibited public worship and evangelisation. The Methodist church building had been taken over for use as a marionette theatre, and the new government had only recently given a site for a brand new church as repayment for what had been confiscated. Donald spoke at the turf-cutting service for the new church, and World Methodist Council visitors gave the local Methodists almost $3,000 in a special offering for their new building. Eddie Fox, Methodist Director of World Evangelism, provides an interesting sequel to this event. When the communists closed the church they removed both the cross and the bell from the tower, but three young men from the church retrieved the bell and buried it in a garden. Thirty years later when the church was recovered the bell was dug up and installed in the new tower. However, it took ten years, from 1992, for the Methodists in Varna to complete the building of the new Methodist church. This was done through the help of World Methodist Evangelism and in September 2002 the church bell, rung by Eddie Fox and the Methodist Superintendent, Bedros Altunian, again called the people of Varna to worship.

Another moving ceremony in Varna at which Donald presided and spoke was the presentation of the 1992 World Methodist Peace Award to Pastor Zdravko Beslov. Born in 1910, he had been appointed pastor of the Methodist church in the Bulgarian capital, Sofia, in 1947, but instead of assuming his new pastoral role he had been imprisoned for fourteen years because of his opposition to the communist regime. Even after being freed he had been kept under constant secret police surveillance, and only in 1989 had he been able to resume his public ministry as a pastor in Sofia and the Superintendent of the Methodist work in Bulgaria. Unable to preach his inaugural sermon back in 1947, he had preached at his first service in 1989 from notes he had prepared forty-two years earlier.[2] At the time of receiving the Peace Award, Pastor Beslov was very frail, and he died only a few months later.

* * * * *

Only eight months after receiving the letter from Mexico complaining about Roman Catholic attitudes and practices, Donald was able to fit in a visit to see things for himself, again accompanied by Joe Hale. The visit took place in January 1993, and gave the opportunity to meet with representatives of various Protestant denominations to hear about their experiences of religious persecution in a country dominated by Catholicism. Donald was horrified that the meeting was constantly interrupted by telephone calls from the Office for Religion at the Mexico Department of State, concerning an incident where, despite a court ruling that a particular town's only Protestant church (an independent Pentecostal congregation) could legally open, groups of local people and town officials had destroyed the building. The Methodist Church at this time was in the process of applying for official recognition and registration under the Mexican government's new legislation for church–state relationships, and Donald was also able to meet with the leaders responsible for presenting that application. He commented: 'I was very impressed with the integrity of the Methodists carrying this responsibility and the quality of their work. They understood the long and complicated history of the place of the church in Mexico ... and were clear about what the Methodist contribution should be.'

---

[2] Reported in *World Parish*, November–December 1992.

Donald's next major visit of that year, following a meeting with Dr Konrad Raiser, General Secretary of the World Council of Churches in Geneva and attendance at the Methodist Conference for Central and Southern Europe in Switzerland in March, was in September, to the Far East, once again accompanied by Joe Hale.[3] Beginning in Hong Kong, they had wide-ranging discussions with pastors and lay people about anticipated changes in 1997, when Hong Kong would return from British to Chinese rule, and together they explored some of the apprehensions felt in view of previous generations' experience of the Cultural Revolution and potential problems over the freedom of religion under the new regime. It was significant, however, that none of those present said they wanted to leave Hong Kong. In response to the question 'What is the policy for mission on the Chinese mainland?' Donald said: 'It is a basic principle that those nearest to the people ought to do the mission. Usually missionary work means travelling away from home, but Christians in Hong Kong are going to find the mission travelling to them.'

From Hong Kong they flew to Malaysia, a country with a Methodist membership of some 100,000 and work extending throughout the Malay Peninsula and into Sarawak. At a meeting of church leaders in Kuala Lumpur, Donald spoke on the subject of unity in the Christian church, and the need to understand how people came to faith in Jesus Christ in the light of the different ways we function as human beings. 'The question is', he said, 'whether or not Jesus Christ is in our lives. People are different: some respond to the preaching of the evangelical message; some to social caring; some to political struggle; others out of concern for the environment or creation. All these concerns have their root in the gospel ... A variety of approaches is needed in order to reach the largest number of people outside the church.'

[3] Reported in *World Parish*, September–October 1993.

Singapore was the next port of call, where among other things the WMC visitors were anxious to hear suggestions from those who had hosted the 1991 World Methodist Conference that might help those planning the next conference scheduled for Brazil in 1996. Each Conference built upon the last, and it was important that experience should be passed on to successive host countries. Other activities in Singapore included addressing students at an impressive new £24 million Anglo-Chinese school and discussing the role of education in Singapore with the school administrators. Donald then went on to address a ministers' meeting on politics and religion and how the church should handle social issues. 'If our proclamation is only about the world', he said, 'we betray the gospel; but if it is only about Jesus we betray the world.'

The final country visited on this Far Eastern tour was Indonesia, a vast area with a population of 182 million people spread over 14,000 islands. Donald and Joe Hale stayed in Jakarta, the capital city. A major topic for discussion was the continuing problem over human rights in East Timor, a matter that had been raised during the 1991 World Methodist Conference, and the WMC Officers met with Dr Sularso Sopatar, General Chair of the Communion of Churches in Indonesia. He insisted that the riots and deaths were not caused by religious conflict, despite the tension existing between Roman Catholic and Protestant communions in East Timor, but by guerrilla activity both by those favouring integration with Indonesia and those wanting independence from it.

A great banquet brought the Indonesian visit to a close. Methodists from throughout Jakarta brought food, and after the meal Donald spoke on 'The Pattern for Mission in the New Testament'. Churches in Jakarta were not having an easy time. As somebody said, 'If people want to build a mosque they just do it; but if it's a church building we have to ask everybody in the community.' Nevertheless, what Donald shared encouraged them greatly, and in the ensuing discussion ideas were shared for more high-visibility events to further the re-establishment of Methodist work in the city.

On the other side of the world, Donald and Bertha English, along with Joe and Mary Hale, paid a special visit on 11 November 1993 to the home of Billy Graham and his wife, Ruth, in Montreat, North Carolina.[4] The Englishes were in the USA for a series of lectures on seminary campuses and in local churches. Although Donald had met Billy Graham on a number of occasions previously, most recently at the enthronement of George Carey as Archbishop of Canterbury, and had actively supported his crusades in Britain, he wanted to make this official visit to strengthen links. As he put it:

> Having met with Pope John Paul II last year at the Vatican and Dr Konrad Raiser, General Secretary of the World Council of Churches, earlier this year in Geneva, we felt it important also to meet with Dr Graham, whose work gave rise to the Lausanne Committee for World Evangelisation, and whose influence has been felt in most parts of the world. As the greatest evangelist of our time he has demonstrated courage throughout his ministry by proclaiming the gospel implications of the life and work of Jesus which touch people personally. Dr Graham has also increasingly shown the relevance of evangelistic preaching to the struggle for social and political justice in the world.

While the three ministers discussed the state of world evangelisation, Donald and Joe sharing with Billy Graham news of developments in Methodist World Evangelism, their spouses met to share matters of mutual interest: Bertha English described her work as a teacher in Britain and the

---

[4] Reported in *World Parish*, November–December 1993.

urgent missionary challenge it presented; Mary Hale spoke of her work as Director of Children's Ministries in an American United Methodist church; and Ruth Graham shared memories of growing up in China and her work as an author and speaker.

The following month saw Donald again flying east, this time to Bombay, India, to chair a meeting of the WMC officers. In another of his masterly and wide-ranging addresses he surveyed the breakdown of the great world powers and the growing search for alternative power blocs; the rise of intense nationalism and the restrictions being placed on population movement; the ethical problems raised by developments in science, technology and medicine; and the search for answers as to what life is really about. He concluded by asserting that the Christian doctrines of creation, incarnation, redemption and judgement provided the only sound basis for a response to the intricate problems facing humanity today, and challenged the WMC to share such a vision.

* * * * *

1994 was to be an equally busy and demanding year. March found Donald English in the hilly Galilean village of Ibillin, less than an hour's drive from armed roadblocks, for the 1994 World Methodist Peace Award presentation. The recipient this time was a Melkite Catholic priest, an Israeli Palestinian named Father Elias Chacour. As a boy he had seen his Palestinian village destroyed and the land that had belonged to his family for generations confiscated. Nevertheless, he had spent the rest of his life seeking to repair wrongs, believing that forgiveness alone brings healing and peace. Reading the citation, Donald said of him: 'You have shown consistency in the message you have given the world through your writings, your lectures, your appearances on

radio and television, and your meeting with countless visitors
… You have stood for reconciliation in the church and have
opened your arms in this community to embrace Muslims,
Christians and Jews.' Some 1,300 students in the Prophet
Elias Community College that Father Elias Chacour had
established in 1981 for Palestinian, Muslim and Jewish
children stood and cheered him as he received the award.

At the end of June Donald took part in a meeting of the
North American Section of the World Methodist Council –
but from 3,000 miles away![5] He had been invited to be
present at Asbury Theological Seminary, Kentucky, but
there was no space in his diary. Instead he addressed the
meeting for twenty minutes from a studio in Leeds, England,
via a large-screen satellite link-up, following which participants in Kentucky stepped to the microphones and engaged
in a further forty minutes of question and answer. As the
American chair put it, 'Methodists don't "ride the circuit"
any more – we plug into it!'

Donald's next international commitment, in August
1994, was again with young people, for the WMC's Fifth
International Christian Youth Conference on Evangelism
held in Hamburg, Germany, which drew some 750 people
from over 50 nations. For the first time delegates were able to
attend the conference from Eastern Europe, and more than
100 participants came from Estonia, Latvia, Russia,
Ukraine, Poland, Czech Republic, Slovakia, Hungary, Mace-
donia, Bulgaria and Serbia. Donald confessed how moved he
had been: 'How wonderful to see all these countries from the
Eastern region bringing their banners. I was glad I didn't
have to speak after that … I was just unable to speak!' In a
powerful address he spoke about how God was making all
things new, and he challenged the young people to join in
that process, concluding: 'Not to offer everything you have in

---

[5] Reported in *World Parish*, July–August 1994.

the service of God who is making all things new is both a total frustration of life and is dangerous and damaging to us ... I know no better way to use your life.'

The next meeting of the WMC Executive took place at the end of the following month, September 1994, this time in the beautiful old city of Tallinn, the capital of Estonia. Like Bulgaria, this country had been under communist rule during fifty long years of Soviet occupation, and the visitors heard many stirring stories of determination and faith under oppression and persecution. In particular, the story of Alexander Kumm typified the resilience of these people. He had been sentenced to twenty-five years plus an additional five years for 'anti-Soviet propaganda' (though more probably because he was a fearless church leader) and was sent to Siberia. Before his release a Soviet committee came to question him in his prison camp. 'What will be your occupation once you are free?' they asked. His response was simply: 'I will continue the work of being a preacher of Jesus Christ.'

Such stories as this provided a thought-provoking background to the work of the Council, and in his opening address Donald English used the biblical picture of the Body of Christ to remind members that, for all their differences of nationality and culture, they belonged to each other and needed each other. Their debates should not be about scoring points off each other, but about together discerning the mind of Christ.

As was usual at these events, the host church had planned a 'cultural evening' during the week, but on this particular occasion it was overshadowed by the tragic sinking of the ferry boat *Estonia* en route to Helsinki that same morning with the loss of all lives. The ship had left Tallinn the previous night, sailing from a terminal overlooked by the hotel in which the Executive was staying. The event cast a shadow over the whole week, and although the cultural event still went ahead, it took on a very different flavour from that originally planned. The Superintendent of the Estonian Methodist Church, Olav Parnamets, requested that this be a solemn night with no applause. It began with children singing quietly as they entered the hall in threes. A lighted candelabra tied with a black ribbon burned in memory of those lost at sea that day. Several choirs made musical contributions appropriate to the moment, and the evening ended as the Tallinn Methodist Church choir sang 'Nearer my God to Thee', the hymn played at the sinking of the *Titanic*. Donald himself was close to tears as he movingly expressed the deep sympathy of the World Methodist family and led the assembled company in prayer. Later in the week the Executive took up an offering for the families bereaved through the ferry disaster, and a cheque for $1,500 was presented to Olav Parnamets.

But the visit to Tallinn had its happier note. Although what had been the 'mother church of Methodism' in Estonia had been destroyed by Soviet bombs in 1944, now a large plot of land had been purchased for a new complex, which would include a sanctuary area for worship, the first Methodist theological seminary in Estonia (the Baltic Mission Centre) and a soup kitchen to serve the poor and homeless. On the final Saturday, a cold and blustery morning, Donald led the whole Executive to the empty field where the foundation stone was laid and the project dedicated to the glory of God and the service of the gospel. Today a magnificent suite of premises on that site serves the needs of Methodist witness. The centre trains students to work through the Methodist Church not only in Tallinn but in many parts of Northern and Eastern Europe.

* * * * *

1995 was a rather less hectic year for Donald, at least in terms of overseas travel. As this was the year of his retirement, he needed to give time both to handing over his Home Mission responsibilities to his successor, Peter Sutcliffe, and to the domestic demands of moving house from Cheam to Oxfordshire. It would be a mistake, though understandable, to assume that during his chairing of the World Methodist Council Donald had no other responsibilities in Britain; that was far from the case. He remained in charge of the Home Mission work and, although his deputy was able to shoulder the day-to-day affairs,[6] he was in his Westminster office and involved in the work as much as his diary allowed. He also continued with other preaching and speaking opportunities around Britain, and remained a regular and popular contributor on the BBC Radio 4 'Thought for the Day' slot.

Once he and Bertha were happily settled in their new Cotswolds home, Donald was off again. One of the first trips in his so-called 'retirement' (but still with a year of WMC chairing to run) was to the United States, where he unveiled a life-size statue of John Wesley at the Virginia Wesleyan College in Norfolk, Virginia. He took the opportunity to urge the 500 people present to commit themselves to evangelism as Wesley had done, and to recapture the original spark of his vision. 'This statue', he said, 'poses us the question: What structure would a church have which took evangelism seriously? What shape would a church be which believed that one of its prime tasks was to reach out and declare to all that God loves them and that Christ died for them? And how does that compare with the shape of my church, and yours?' As the college chaplain put it afterwards, 'Dr English challenged us to do more than just maintain our institutions. He's saying that we should not carry on with business as usual.'

October 1995 brought another WMC officers' meeting, this time held in Cambridge, England, at which Donald

---

[6] Brian Hoare had been appointed Deputy General Secretary in September 1990 when Donald became President of the Conference.

again drew members' attention to the importance of the apologetic task and spoke again of 'the Wesley quadrilateral'. The following month, in a letter to Norman (Ned) Dewire, President of the Methodist Theological School in Ohio, USA, and Chair of the WMC's working party on Diversity and Pluralism, he unpacked his thinking further on that topic by way of comment on a section of the working party's draft paper.[7] It is worth quoting in full as it gives a valuable insight into Donald's own theological position:

> There is reference under 'Our Beliefs' to Scripture and the Creeds. But it omits what may be one of John Wesley's greatest contributions to Methodism, namely how to do theology. The importance of the centrality of Scripture is crucial. But so is the fact that Wesley acknowledged the importance of Reason, Tradition and Experience. I don't think it's helpful to refer to this as the Methodist Quadrilateral, because Scripture is meant to be so central and the other three are not equal in terms of content and contribution. I prefer to think in terms of a mobile, with Scripture central and the other three circulating around it. You can only come to Scripture via Reason, Tradition and Experience. At the same time Scripture, in Wesley's thinking, was also the judge of our Reason, Tradition and Experience.
>
> That lively inter-relation is at the heart of true Methodist theological thinking and behaving ... If too much attention is paid to Reason we end up with dry and unrealistic academic reflection. Too much reliance on Tradition can lock us up in the past. Over-concentration on Experience produces fanaticism. Attempts to isolate Scripture lead to superstition. Our struggle has to be constantly to treat Scripture as central, to relate the others to it, and to interrelate them to each other.

* * * * * *

---

[7] Letter dated 1 November 1995.

Donald was on home territory for his first major engagement of 1996, a celebration marking the 50th anniversary of the first General Assembly of the United Nations, held in Westminster Central Hall, London. At the Sunday morning service, televised live by the BBC, he preached to about 2,500 people filling that great auditorium, including the Secretary General of the UN, Dr Boutros-Ghali, ambassadors, Members of Parliament and other distinguished guests. Donald's challenge was clear: 'To dream of belonging to one world family, and to be generous enough to make that possible; to commit ourselves to trust others and to give grounds for being trusted; and to offer ourselves in the creating of a peaceful world.' He concluded: 'Let us walk in the light of the Lord, and stay on this journey together until we walk into peace on earth and goodwill among all people.'

February 1996 saw another World Methodist Peace Award presentation, this time to Bishop Stanley Mogoba in Johannesburg, South Africa.[8] How things had changed since Donald's last visit to South Africa! Stanley Mogoba had himself been one of the agents of that change and his award was greeted with traditional African expressions of unrestrained and exuberant joy. Donald spoke warmly of the Bishop's consistency in never advocating violence or taking sides – white or black, tribal or party political – in the struggle against apartheid. He commended his courage in seeking reconciliation and his determination to work among the churches in Southern Africa as a Methodist leader seeking a way forward in the footsteps of Jesus Christ. Responding, Dr Mogoba confessed that his pilgrimage of peace had not been an easy one:

It was in a tiny cell on Robben Island that I was lifted up from the lowest depth of sorrow and despair. A call to the ministry

---

[8] Reported in *World Parish*, July–August 1996.

was hammered on the anvil of deep and excruciating pain and suffering. Refused a Bible, refused a ministry and pastoral care, sentenced to six lashes for taking part in a hunger strike, followed by many other acts of brutality and humiliation, the call to the ministry persisted.

In the early 1980s Mogoba had been a lone voice calling for reconciliation in South Africa, but his stance had been vindicated as national reconciliation had become the order of the day under a new government headed by one of his fellow prisoners on Robben Island, Nelson Mandela.

*   *   *   *   *

There were other pressing invitations that year, but Donald was by now aware of some of the health problems that were to overshadow his final years. He was clearly saving his energies for the final responsibility of his five-year term of office, the Seventeenth World Methodist Conference to be held in Rio de Janeiro, Brazil, in August 1996.[9] During the summer his heart problems had become more persistent, and there was doubt as to whether he would be able to go to Rio at all. Bertha kept him on a tight rein to prevent any overexertion, and few of the 2,700 conference members at Rio knew that Donald was anything but his old self. If he was physically weakened, all the familiar oratory and spiritual power was there, and his years of leadership were brought to a fitting close as the conference explored its theme 'Holy Spirit – Giver of Life'. One particularly memorable moment came when in the course of debate a speaker from the floor suggested that the WMC was racist. People were greatly moved as Donald responded to the charge and publicly wept at the thought of being guilty of such a thing: his tears were so obviously genuine.

[9] Reported in *World Parish*, September–October 1996.

In his keynote address, Donald said that modern Methodists had much to learn from the early Christians who experienced the Holy Spirit at Pentecost. They had been an obedient people, united in fellowship, committed to praying together as they planned for their future work and witness. He concluded:

> Though their culture and setting were different from ours, they were in many ways just like us, ordinary human beings, full of frailty and the capacity to get it wrong! We are not, of course, on the eve of the first Pentecost as they were. But there is no reason why we should not be on the eve of a new Pentecost when the Holy Spirit descends with renewed vigour for us all. We would wish by God's grace to be ready for that.

Besides chairing the Council sessions, Donald's other major task at the conference was to address a mammoth celebration in the enormous domed Maracananzinho Stadium. More than eighteen thousand Brazilian Methodists, many travelling long distances overnight by bus, joined conference members for a three-hour service featuring a choir of a thousand children, elaborate choreography, joyful Brazilian music and preaching. In his greeting to this huge and colourful gathering, Donald spoke of the unity of Methodist people around the world – now approaching 63 million in well over 100 countries – and of the importance of remaining faithful to the Christian calling and Methodist tradition:

> John Wesley refused to set a limit on what God could achieve in our lives. Nor would he dismiss any life, however evil or poor or unpromising, as a possible avenue of God's free grace. We Methodists are true to our calling in Christ, and to our Methodist inheritance, when we hold to this 'optimism of grace', and in that spirit we celebrate our faith today.

Conference members in Rio were accommodated in comfortable hotels, but none could escape the sight of the huge
favelas (slums) sprawling up the nearby hillsides or the
street children eking out an existence around this teeming
city. Before coming to Rio, conference members had been
asked to prepare for a special collection to be taken during
the stadium rally for the Brazilian Methodism's work
among these street children, and Donald was able to
announce the result four days later. 'I expected the offering
to be large', he said, 'but the amount is much larger than I
thought it would be.' Then, his voice breaking with emotion, he revealed the total: $204,093 had been given.

At the end of the Rio conference, Donald handed over his
badge of office to his successor, Dr Frances Alguire, an
American laywoman, and his term of high office had come to
an end. He received messages of thanks from many people,
known and unknown. One such letter simply said 'Bravo!
Bravo! Bravo! You used outstanding skill as our Chairperson. Praise the Lord, and thank your physician, for saving
your energy and health so you could lead us.' Joe Hale, the
WMC General Secretary with whom Donald had worked so
closely, wrote:

> What an incredible privilege and joy it has been to be associ-
> ated with you this past five years! But even more, our lives have
> been linked for all the time I have known much about the
> World Methodist Council – from the time we moved here in
> 1975 and you knew you would be leading the Bible studies in
> Dublin, stretching all the way to the present time and, with you
> as Honorary President of the Council, through that veiled
> curtain that separates us from the future to the end when we
> 'cast our crowns before him, lost in wonder, love and praise'.[10]

---

[10] J. Hale to D. English, 19 September 1996.

11

Donald English – Himself

We have charted Donald English's life and ministry
throughout the chapters of this book. But what kind of man
was he? What sort of personality lay behind all that he
accomplished? Thousands saw him in public; but what was
he like in private?[1] A tall, slim, pleasant-featured man with
upright bearing and athletic figure, neatly and soberly
dressed, his once sandy-red hair was latterly thinning and
grey, giving him a distinguished look. People were immediately put at ease by his open and friendly face, smiling eyes
and the welcoming grip of a large freckled hand out-
stretched in greeting. He was well spoken with a softly lilt-
ing voice that gave just a hint of his north-eastern roots and
was instantly recognisable to thousands who never met him
in person but listened avidly to his regular radio broadcasts
or heard him on tape.

Graphologists would have had a field day reading
Donald's character from his handwriting! It always had a
flow to it; one word often joined to another by a sweeping
stroke of the pen. Over the years it seemed to gather a growing urgency and become increasingly illegible, as if he was a
man in a hurry whose pen could not keep up with his fertile

---

[1] Some of the material in this chapter first appeared in B. Hoare,
'Donald English – Himself' in Abbott (ed.), *Donald English*,
pp. 38–40.

mind. This was partly due to the mounting pressure of responsibility he shouldered, but was also indicative of the vision that drove him onwards. He was, as we have seen, a man of firm evangelical conviction, a sharp and incisive thinker, and a strong personality who knew what he was aiming for and would leave no stone unturned to achieve it. Some misinterpreted his determination as personal ambition. Whilst 'ambitious' is certainly a word that could be justly applied to him, and he did seek and grasp opportunities to influence (even to steer) people and events, his ambition was always ultimately for the good of the church and the further-ance of the gospel rather than for any sort of personal aggrandisement. The whole dynamic 'flow' of his life was for the greater glory of God.

Donald was a man of deep Christian commitment and disciplined personal devotion. His personal Bible study not only fed him as an individual, but also provided him with countless devotional gems to pass on to others in the course of his working day. Again and again those who sat under his chairmanship in committees and meetings would hear as he led opening devotions: 'In my Bible reading this morning I was struck by …' A brief exposition often illustrated by a memorable story or quotation would follow. Prayer too was of vital importance to him. On one occasion, at a Home Mission staff meeting, his colleagues were moved to hear him say: 'I'm always grateful that the walk from Victoria Station to Westminster Central Hall is just long enough to pray for every member of staff by name each morning.'

Donald's prayer support was sought and valued not only by those who shared his faith, but by others too. One morn-ing he was awoken by the telephone ringing at about 4.00am. It was Ray Grady, a non-churchgoing neighbour who lived opposite Donald and Bertha in Anne Boleyn's Walk, Cheam. His wife, Eve, was critically ill in the Atkinson Morley hospital. Ray was not a praying man himself, but he asked if Donald would go to the hospital to pray with her. It happened to be a day on which Donald was doing one of his Radio 4 'Thought for the Day' talks, and a car would be arriving at 5.00am to take him to the studio. He therefore rang Michael Whelton, one of the ministers at the church where he and Bertha worshipped, and asked him to become involved. Donald promised that he would pray for Eve Grady as he travelled to London. Michael Whelton takes up the story:

> I arrived at the hospital and was met by the ward sister who said that Eve had an inoperable tumour and that death was close. She was unconscious and the doctors and nurses moved aside as I ministered to her. Miraculously Eve recovered. Since her recovery she and Ray, her husband, have totally committed their lives to Christ. They are now members and regular worshippers at Cheam Methodist Church and use every opportunity to spread the news of God's healing grace. They praise and thank God for the intervention and prayers of Don English.

Commitment to private prayer was seen by Donald as crucially important; so too was corporate worship. Although open to new ideas and second to none in his insistence that we are called 'to serve the present age' and to incarnate the gospel in our own time and culture, Donald was nevertheless a traditionalist at heart. He enjoyed singing contemporary worship songs, but would more naturally choose the tried-and-tested hymns of the faith when leading worship himself. He liked things done properly, and enjoyed the formal ceremonial that characterised events such as the opening of the Methodist Conference. Donald combined a sense of dignity with personal warmth, in worship and in other settings. It is interesting to note that until his designation as President in 1978 he had always been known as

'Don', but from then on his signature became 'Donald'. Perhaps he deemed that to be more 'proper'!

Those who saw him only in more formal settings might not have realised that the real Donald was a fun-loving, outgoing person, with a great sense of humour and funny stories for every occasion. His Geordie upbringing had somehow given him a belief in the importance of the ordinary, and he revelled in being with ordinary people, doing ordinary things and enjoying ordinary pleasures. His love of sport has already been noted. He enjoyed good food, though had fairly traditional tastes, and he and Bertha loved entertaining others in their home. He would relax by listening to music, especially his beloved Mozart (of whose works he had a considerable collection), and loved wandering round art galleries and museums. He read immensely widely in all sorts of fields besides theology, and particularly enjoyed biographies, of which he had an impressive number in his library. As his son Richard observes:

> It was always the people behind the books – whether subject or author – in which he was primarily interested. He read books to get to people, and especially to individuals. Dad himself always saw people as individuals, and part of his gift was to treat everyone he met in terms of their individual dignity and uniqueness. Again and again in the letters people wrote to me after his death this was what they said: that he always treated them as special, as unique, as if they were distinctive in his eyes.

Indeed, to get to know Donald English was to discover someone who was genuinely 'a friend to all and the enemy of none', as Wesley put it. He had the knack of making people feel they mattered, and in conversation would give them his undivided attention. This even extended to those with whom he profoundly disagreed, for he was always gracious. A former student of Donald's said: 'Donald's nature was to love, and he was more accepting of people's foibles and failings than any man I have ever met. He did, however, on one occasion say to us students: "Oh, occasionally I have been tempted to offer the right knee of fellowship!" ' Donald was an encourager, who made people believe in themselves.

Above all other relationships, it was his family that brought Donald the greatest pleasure of all. He was immensely proud of his two sons, Richard (now Professor of Politics at Queens University, Belfast) and Paul (Chief Executive of swotbooks.com and Managing Director of IPL Consulting), and their wives, Maxine and Carol, and took great delight in his grandchildren. He was totally devoted to Bertha, and they were demonstrably affectionate when together. Whenever Donald was away on his travels Bertha's photograph always stood on his bedside table and he would ring her every night to share the day's news.

Although family time was always vitally important to Donald, he often struggled to carve it out of his diary in the midst of a busy life. As a teenager during the Bristol years, Richard used to book tickets for orchestral concerts at the Colston Hall every six weeks or so, thus ensuring that his father reserved time in his diary for the family on those nights. As Richard put it: 'Maybe it says something about his approach: he was so busy that we had to try to book him, yet he was prepared to be booked and always enjoyed those family times together.'

Something else that enabled Donald to spend time with his boys was their mutual love of football. One particular memory recalled by Paul illustrates how the family worked together to make the most of family time as well as supporting Donald's calling to preach.

It was the 1985 FA Cup Final (always a traditional family occasion in front of the TV) between Manchester United and

Everton. In discussing the lead up to the event, Dad realised that he had a preaching engagement late on the afternoon of the game, and would have to miss the match to travel into central London. The idea of watching the Cup Final without him was anathema, and so the family made the trip up to Westminster Central Hall and rigged up a television in his office so that we could all enjoy the event together prior to his preaching appointment. On reflection, there are a large number of illustrations of family sacrifice for the life Dad was compelled to follow, but I can honestly say that at the time it did not occur to me once that this was cumbersome. It was such a natural part of the family's values that it was never once questioned. How could anything possibly be put before Mum and Dad's commitment to serve God? The family simply rallied to support it.

Another enjoyable form of relaxation for Donald whenever he had the time was gardening – though that was never as often as he would have liked. He worked furiously and lovingly on the Cheam garden whenever he had the chance, and would have his radio with him, listening either to Radio 4 or perhaps to the sports channel if it was a Saturday or if there was cricket or football commentary on that day.

Early on in their time in Cheam, Donald and Bertha bought their dog, Abigail (or Abi as she was more commonly called), and Donald loved to walk her in the local park at the end of the road. The sight of him wandering off down the road with the devoted Abi, a golden retriever, at his side became a familiar one in the locality. Whenever they could take Abi with them on their travels, Donald and Bertha did so, but when that was not possible she went to stay with Jill Edmonds (née Andrews), their friend from Nigeria days. Jill noted that when the Englishes first had Abi as a puppy, she slept at night in her basket in the garage, but then she progressed to the kitchen, then to a special chair and finally into the bedroom! Donald doted on Abi, and it was not long before she became much more widely known as the subject of frequent sermon illustrations. Joe Hale remembers one of them:

> In his Bible studies Donald often introduced other theologians and eminent persons. The most memorable, however, was his dog, Abigail! 'We have a golden retriever puppy in our family, and I'm discovering some very interesting things about dogs. The first is they have a kind of selective deafness. When I see Abigail doing something wrong in the garden I go to the door and I say 'Abi', but she doesn't hear. She just stands, looking ahead. But if I say 'Food, Abi', she hears! And if she comes in and she's done something wrong, I say, 'Abigail, what have you been doing?' and she studies the ground; so I lift her nose up towards me so that our eyes are always meeting, and she is looking here and here, and here. What she will not do is look me straight in the face. Even dogs know what sin is!

Donald always had a great capacity to relax: he had a very stressful job, with much pressure and many responsibilities, but he had the invaluable ability to switch off when it was time to do so. He could do this for brief periods (when listening to music, watching football on television or walking the dog in the park), but he could also do so for longer stretches when on holiday. For that reason family holidays were especially treasured times. Richard recalls three successive holidays in Culdaff, County Donegal, Ireland, which he and his wife Maxine spent with his parents, staying in a house owned by a good friend of theirs of many years, Paul Kingston, a former Nigeria missionary and now Donald's opposite number in the Methodist Church in Ireland. Says Richard:

> I remember both Mum and Dad being strikingly relaxed on these holidays. Donegal was the opposite, I suppose, of his

London life. They were then living in Cheam, and Dad commuted most days up to Westminster Central Hall. Looking out over the beautiful beach at Culdaff, he used often to say that he would store up the image of this restful place by the sea and remember it when crossing the concourse again at Victoria station once the holiday was over. I remember him swimming most days in the sea in Donegal – a courageous act for anyone given the coldness of the water! He wanted to be part of the fun and so we all went in, splashed about and then thankfully warmed up back in the house with a cup of tea, cosy again after our family dip in the Atlantic. This when he was in his sixties!

When Donald retired in the summer of 1995 he and Bertha moved to Shipton-under-Wychwood, a village in Oxfordshire where they had previously bought a house. They loved both the house and the area, not least because of the proximity of other family members: Paul and Carol lived nearby, and so did Bertha's sister, Aileen, with her husband, John, and their daughter, Anne. Although they were moving to a new place, therefore, they did have loved ones already close by. Carol recalls:

Don spent a great deal of time helping look after his grandchildren. At the time our second child, Sam, was born Lucy (our first) was only 15 months old. Paul was working away from home in the week and Don became a very willing and practical source of help for us. I would take the children to his house in Shipton at 10.00am so we could all watch *Teletubbies* together. Don would always have been round to the local village shop to buy a Kit-Kat each to have with our coffee or juice. At teatime, Don would wherever possible arrive at our house to help with baths for what he called the 'five o'clock shift'. I have a clear memory of him walking in the garden with Lucy while I bathed Sam. They would be picking up feathers or stones and having great discussions. It always amused me to see Don's diary, which could include meetings with archbishops and government ministers alongside reminders about Lucy and Sam's bath and teatimes.

Carol English continues:

Don enjoyed seeing his sons' families together too. We have fond memories of a weekend early in the summer in which he died when we spent a day visiting Stratford with Richard's family too. Jasmine, Richard's eldest, used to refer to Don as her 'Ra-Ra', since Grandpa was a bit of a mouthful. Our Lucy used instead to call him her 'Ba-Ba'. Don used to joke that 'Ga-Ga' might have been more appropriate for him! Don was certainly much more than a father-in-law to me. He always involved himself in the normal, everyday routines of life, despite his elevated position within the church. When he died, I remember feeling that in many ways I had lost my 'best friend' and life would never be the same for any of us.

*   *   *   *   *

Donald and Bertha looked forward with great anticipation in 1995 to a long and happy retirement in their new home. Sadly that was not to be. Nevertheless, there were good times in the Shipton-under-Wychwood years. The neighbours and friends in the close where Donald and Bertha lived were wonderful: welcoming, kind and good fun. They enjoyed too the worship and fellowship of the little Methodist church in nearby Burford, and Donald's preaching in the chapels of this rural circuit was greatly appreciated. A particularly high moment came when Donald was appointed a CBE in the 1996 Queen's Birthday Honours list. This meant a trip to Buckingham Palace (by no means for the first time in Donald's case) where, on 17 October 1996, the investiture took place and Her Majesty Queen Elizabeth II made him a

Commander of the British Empire – the highest of the three non-knighthood orders. The citation indicated that the award had been given 'for service to World Methodism', but it was recognised that this was really the culmination of a lifetime's distinguished and devoted service to Methodism as a whole.

Despite that highlight, however, and the stimulus of the WMC Conference in Rio de Janeiro, 1996 was a difficult year. Donald had been unwell earlier in the year, and a medical examination revealed a heart problem, which required an operation to fit a pacemaker. John Barratt, a Methodist minister who was headmaster of The Leys School, Cambridge, and a member of the WMC Presidium, recalls their time together when the Conference was over:

> After the Rio WMC Conference, Donald and Bertha and Sally [John Barratt's wife] and I found we had independently planned to stay on for a week's holiday. So we spent much of the time together, sightseeing and resting. Donald was recovering from his heart operation and, although he had tried to pace himself, was very tired following the Conference. Bertha was very concerned for his health, and on several occasions insisted that one of us rest with Donald while the other two continued on a walk or a climb. Ironically, it was Bertha's health we should have been more concerned about. She gave the odd hint she was not well, but brushed it off as nothing serious. When she got home, tests revealed that she had cancer, and she died a year later.

It was in October 1996 that Bertha really began to feel ill. She was eventually diagnosed as having cancer of the liver and Donald brought her home from hospital with only a few days to live. In the event she lived for a further three months, still weak, but able to enjoy her food, to sit in a wheelchair in the garden or even to have occasional trips out in the car. It was during this period that both Donald and Bertha were greatly helped by visits from 'Jeff' Jefferies of the Pin Mill Christian Healing Fellowship in Felixstowe, Suffolk, who laid hands on her, prayed for her and offered counselling. Reflecting on the experience some months after Bertha's death, Donald wrote an article for *Life-Line*, the Pin Mill journal, entitled 'The Experience of Healing'. It contained some of the most personal and revealing things he ever wrote, and a few quotations from the article give something of its flavour:

Prayer and the laying on of hands made a difference. We saw physical improvements on a number of occasions after such ministry. Why some are healed and others are not I have no idea. But then neither do I know why some people are so much cleverer than I, why some can sing and I can't, why I was raised in such a happy home when others were not, and so on. There are descriptions of 'how' this is so, but I am concerned with the 'why'. I find myself going back to the question of the vineyard owner in Matthew 20 who, when asked why he was paying all his workers according to need rather than hours worked, replied 'Am I not free to do what I please with what is my own? Or are you jealous because I am generous?'

There were times during Bertha's illness, and there have been for me since, when the signals of divine presence were deeply surprising as well as comforting and challenging. At times such signals were almost overpowering, not least on two occasions involving a vision of the risen Christ in the room. (I don't find that easy to write, since I am not a person whose Christian life has been marked by such experiences.) More ordinarily we would sometimes begin a day when so many things had to happen and so many people came to visit us that we wondered how we would possibly get through. We discovered it was as though someone outside was lining people up and ushering them in – and out – on cue! Then there were the frequent emphases of the same scripture text or theological reflection by a variety of people who didn't even know one another. I realise that to some this may seem rather trivial and not very profound. In our situation it was a constant reminder that 'Underneath are the everlasting arms' and that 'God is at work in all things for good with those who love him'. That knowledge was the deepest healing of all, which we both received and by the strength of which we were both sustained.

What follows next is the hardest thing for me to put into words without sounding trite or presumptuous. It is simply how relevant the life, death and resurrection of Jesus are to the experience of illness and pain felt both by the patient and the loved one ... The sense that there are footsteps ahead along the road, made by Jesus himself, can be of profound comfort and strength; not least when one remembers that the journey he made ended not just in the darkness of death but eventually in the light of resurrection. Such understanding doesn't remove the darkness, pain and heartbreak involved. The valley of the shadow of death remains a truly awful place. But it does provide light at the end of the valley, enabling one to know joy even when happiness seems to have fled for ever.[2]

Bertha's death, on 23 July 1997, was a bitter blow for the whole family, but a devastating one for Donald. Their son Richard wrote:

Dad cared for Mum tenderly during these Shipton years, first as her health required attention and diagnosis, and then as she faced serious illness and ultimately death. In some ways, the most central theme in Dad's life as I witnessed it over the years was his love for Mum, and this was reflected both in the loving kindness he showed in her last months, and in the emotional shell shock with which her death left him. It wasn't that he couldn't deal with what had happened: his faith and his personal strength left him well able to carry on robustly and vigorously. But a part of him, naturally enough, died when she did.

[2] *Life-Line*, 30 April 1998.

Richard's brother Paul made a similar observation, writing:

> When Mum died, I was relieved to live only five minutes away
> from my Dad. I visited him every night for a chat and a hot
> chocolate to reflect on the day and talk through how he was
> feeling. Some evenings we just sat and held hands when words
> were unnecessary or inadequate. It was in this period that the
> enormity of my Mum's loss to him became apparent. He
> would refer to the fact that when things happened there was no
> one to tell. He said he would have to learn the value of things
> for their own sake, rather than in the relaying of them to Mum.
> I had always seen him as a uniquely strong and independent
> man, but now for the first time I realised that she was his point
> of reference. Whatever happened to him, happened in the
> context of *them*. This was a special and close time, but also one
> of discovery for me. Only in my Mum's death did I really come
> to understand this aspect of my father.

Bertha was buried on 28 July, their wedding anniversary.
Among the many letters Donald received after Bertha's death
was one from Brian Greet, former Chair of the Nottingham
and Derby District, referring to the theme of the manna
provided for the Israelites in the wilderness and how helpful
a picture it provided of God's unfailing provision with each
returning day. Donald wrote in reply: 'The theme of the
manna which you mentioned has become quite fundamental
to my survival and well-being. It was mentioned in last
Sunday morning's Radio 4 worship from Walsingham and
the Shrine of Our Lady (not quite my cup of tea!). But it
struck me so forcibly as the pattern of my life now. Thank
you for reinforcing it.' [3]

In that same letter Donald also referred briefly to himself,
for his own health had been giving further cause for
concern: 'As far as my health is concerned, the tests so far

[3] Letter dated 16 August 1997.

are clear, with one to go. I think I probably just need an extended rest, and I am going to try to take that once the month of August is over.' However, that proved an over-optimistic assessment of the situation, and over the coming months his heart condition deteriorated further to the point that eventually a triple bypass was going to be needed. Donald continued to take on some preaching engagements but was very selective about what he under-took. Those who attended the packed ordination service in York Minster during the Scarborough Methodist Confer-ence in July 1998 will long remember his powerful sermon on that occasion. It was one of the last he preached. He had also been the guest preacher for The Leys School speech day on Saturday 27 June 1998. The school's headmaster, John Barratt, describes the occasion:

> Donald was not well, and it was known that he had to go into hospital shortly, but out of personal friendship he insisted on coming to fulfil the engagement. He was preaching mainly to those who were leaving school that day. His theme was that there is more to life than scientific materialism may be aware of. He was urging sixth formers to look beyond that which is secular to that which may be described as spiritual. In his final point he spoke about life beyond death. 'I do not believe', he said, 'that this world is all that there is, or that death is the end.' He referred to Bertha's death, and his conviction that she was still alive with God. With tears in his eyes and a crack in his voice, he went on: 'The veil between this world and the next is gossamer thin, and I cannot wait to pass through it.' Just a few weeks later he did.

The major heart surgery at the John Radcliffe Hospital in Oxford appeared to have gone well and Donald was making good progress, being sent to a local cottage hospital to recuperate. Richard came over from Belfast, and describes in moving terms what happened next:

The week before he died, I went to bring Dad out of hospital following his heart operation, for what should have been a recovery at home. This was August 1998 and he was in a hospital in Chipping Norton when I arrived in England, so I went to see him and to arrange to take him home. He was asleep in a chair by his bed when I got there and, at first, he didn't know I was there. He looked far from well. I was in two minds as to whether I should wake him, but he must have sensed that someone had come into the room, I suppose, and he slowly opened his eyes and smiled his warm, wise, kind smile, and we embraced in love and in greeting. I remember him in those terms: loving, kind, wise, warm, deeply humane and – that rare combination – both very talented and very humble. He was highly intelligent, and he was great company and he was a very funny man to spend time with. A son remembering his dead father is always in danger of exaggerating the man's strengths and good qualities. But in saying that Dad was a very special person, I think I'm saying something that will be understood by many people who had the privilege of knowing him. He was the loveliest man I've ever met.

* * * * * *

The untimely death of Donald English on 28 August 1998 hit the Methodist world like a bolt from the blue. People simply could not believe that he was gone, and that within only three years of his retirement, and still with so much to offer, both he and his wife were dead. Five weeks later, on Friday 2 October 1998, over a thousand people gathered in Westminster Central Hall for a service of thanksgiving for his life and ministry. It was a stirring occasion with glorious music and spoken tributes from a galaxy not only of Methodist church leaders but others too: Cardinal Basil Hume, the Bishop of Lambeth (representing the Archbishop of Canterbury), John Reardon (Secretary of the

Council of Churches in Britain and Ireland), Geoffrey Roper (Secretary of the Free Church Federal Council), and with tributes read from Joe Hale (WMC General Secretary), Frances Alguire (Donald's successor as WMC Chair), Billy Graham and Cardinal Cassidy (Pontifical Council for Promoting Christian Unity). Billy Graham's tribute referred to Donald as 'one of the greatest men of God I have ever known', and continued: 'There are few men in the ministry of any denomination that I have looked up to and wanted to emulate like Don English. It is my prayer that God will raise up other men like him not only to lead and influence World Methodism but the entire world church.' Yet for those who gathered there, and for the many others who were touched by his life, it was not so much Donald's achievements and honours that they remembered, impressive though they were. It was rather the person he was: Donald the man, whose life illustrated so well the faith he lived and preached, and who somehow made it so much easier for others to believe in Jesus too.

After the memorial service at the Central Hall one of Donald's friends from student days, John C. Newton, bumped into Michael Griffiths, who had been a colleague of Donald's on the IVF staff, and who later led the Overseas Missionary Fellowship and London Bible College. As they reminisced together, Newton recalls Griffiths commenting: 'My, we have come a long way. Cardinals on the platform! Who would have believed it?' That comment spoke volumes about the changes in the ecclesiastical landscape since the 1950s, and Donald English was one who had played a significant part in bringing those changes about.

Perhaps in this sense it is wrong to divide Donald the person from his achievements. It was his outstanding gift for relationships with other people that enabled him to be such an effective pastor. His deep personal allegiance to Christ and his commitment to Scripture was what was communicated in his ministry, whether when working with students, as a theological teacher, or as a preacher and evangelist. He was one of the best Christian communicators of his generation. Donald was also a fine thinker and was always open to new ideas. This was evident in the way he listened to Christians who had different perspectives, for example on political and social action. He was a key figure in the broadening of evangelical thinking in the second half of the twentieth century. His wide sympathies made him an ideal person to further ecumenical enterprise. Finally, because he gained such enormous respect for who he was as well as what he did, he could become a highly effective World Methodist statesman.

A memorial window to Don and Bertha was commissioned for Wesley's Chapel in City Road, London. This was painted by Mark Cazalet, and has as its theme – expressed through five engraved pictures – the motif of God as fire. The aim of the window, as the *Methodist Recorder* of 31 May 2001 reported, was to celebrate the life of a man and his wife 'dedicated to evangelising, encouraging and building up the Church'. Furthermore, visitors to Westminster Central Hall today, the scene of that great service of thanksgiving and Donald's office base for the last thirteen years of his active ministry, will find one of the newly refurbished conference rooms named 'The Donald English Room'. It is used for a wide variety of activities and functions, Methodist, ecumenical and secular – a telling reminder that Donald himself was so much more than a Methodist. A life that had begun in very unremarkable surroundings had turned out to be a very remarkable life indeed.

Appendix 1

Important dates in the life of Donald English

20 July 1930	Donald English born in Consett
1948–53	Student at University College, Leicester
1953–5	National Service in the Royal Air Force
1955–8	Travelling Secretary for the Inter-Varsity Fellowship
1958–60	Student at Wesley House, Cambridge
1960–2	Assistant Tutor at Wesley College, Headingley, Leeds
1962	Married Bertha Forster Ludlow
1963	Richard English born
1962–5	New Testament Tutor at Union Theological College, Umuahia, Nigeria
1965	Paul English born
1966–72	Minister, Cullercoats Methodist Church
1972–3	Tutor in Historical Theology, Hartley Victoria College, Manchester
1973–82	Tutor in Practical Theology and Methodism, Wesley College, Bristol
1978–9	President of the Methodist Conference
1982–95	General Secretary of the Methodist Home Mission Division
1986–7	Moderator of the Free Church Federal Council
1990–1	President of the Methodist Conference
1991–6	Chairman of the World Methodist Council
1996	Awarded a CBE
28 August 1998	Donald English died

Appendix 2

Bibliography of books and booklets by Donald English

Evangelism and Worship (Methodist Home Mission Department, 1971)

God in the Gallery (Epworth Press, 1975)

Christian Discipleship the Hard Way (Studies in Mark's Gospel; Methodist Publishing House, 1977)

Windows on the Passion (Epworth Press, 1978)

From Wesley's Chair (Epworth Press, 1979)

Anything to Declare? Reflections on Telling Others about the Faith (London Baptist Preachers' Association, 1980)

Sharing in God's Mission (Methodist Home Mission Division, 1985)

Why Believe in Jesus? (Epworth Press, 1986)

Evangelistic Counselling (Methodist Home Mission Division, 1987)

Evangelism Now (Methodist Home Mission Division, 1987)

The Meaning of the Warmed Heart (Methodist Home Mission Division, 1987 and Discipleship Resources USA, 1987)

Caring and the Struggle for Justice (Methodist Home Mission Division, 1988)

Everything In Christ: Lenten Studies in Colossians (Bible Reading Fellowship, 1988)

The Heart of the Matter: Five Studies on the death of Jesus (Methodist Home Mission Division, 1991)

The Message of Mark (Inter-Varsity Press, 1992)

Christianity and Politics (Queen's University of Belfast Department of Politics, 1993)

Into the 21st Century (Methodist Home Mission Division, 1995)

An Evangelical Theology of Preaching (Abingdon Press, 1996)

Edited books and contributory chapters

'The Bible and Contemporary Issues', in John Job (ed.), *Studying God's Word* (Inter-Varsity Press, 1972)

'Faith in the New Testament', in John Stacey (ed.), *About Faith* (Local Preachers' Department of the Methodist Church, 1972)

'Ministry and Ordination', in Kenneth Wilson (ed.), *The Experience of Ordination* (Epworth Press, 1979)

'Complete in Christ – Studies in Philippians', in David Porter (ed.), *The People and the King* (Keswick Convention Council, 1980)

'A Warm Heart and a Humble Mind – Studies in 1 Peter', in David Porter (ed.), *God's Very Own People* (Keswick Convention Council, 1984)

'Bridging the Gap', in Edward England (ed.), *My Call to Preach* (Highland, 1986)

'Privilege and Responsibility', in Vicky Cosstick (ed.), *Aids – Meeting the Community Challenge* (St Paul, 1987)

'John Wesley – Evangelist', in Roland C. Gibbons (ed.), *What hath God Wrought* (Grenville, 1988)

'Called to be Saints – Studies in 1 Corinthians', in David Porter (ed.), *Real People – Real Faith* (Keswick Convention Council, 1988)

Ten Praying Churches (ed.) (Monarch, 1989)

'Jesus Christ as "The Word" in John 1 and Evangelism', in Martin Forward (ed.), *God of all Faith* (Methodist Home Mission Division, 1989)

'Science, Religion and Apologetics in the 1990s', in Kenneth Wilson (ed.), *Interpreting the Cosmos* (Christ and the Cosmos, 1992)

'The Life of Faith – Paul's Letter to the Galatians', in David Porter (ed.), *Dangerous Faith* (Keswick Convention Council, 1993)

'The Search for the Truth', in David Brodie and Rachel McConnell (eds), *Selected Sermons for Christian Students on Campus* (The Edwin Mellen Press, 1993)

Windows on Salvation (ed.) (Darton, Longman & Todd, 1994)

Index